KI-L

Oxfordshire
Houses

Oxfordshire Houses

JOHN C. PILLING

OXFORDSHIRE BOOKS

First published in 1993 by Oxfordshire Books

British Library Cataloguing in Publication Data

Pilling, John C.
Oxfordshire Houses
I. Title
728.09425

ISBN 0-7509-0222-1

Library of Congress Cataloging in Publication Data Applied for

OXFORDSHIRE BOOKS
Publishing imprint of
Oxfordshire County Council
Department of Leisure and Arts
in collaboration with
Alan Sutton Publishing Ltd
Phoenix Mill · Far Thrupp · Stroud
Gloucestershire

Typeset in 11/14 Times.
Typesetting and origination by
Alan Sutton Publishing Limited.
Printed and bound in Great Britain by
The Bath Press Ltd, Bath, Avon.

Contents

The open hall of the Manor House, Sutton Courtenay, in the 1920s

Introduction

The historic houses of our towns and countryside have never been under such threat as they are today, and the threat often comes from overzealous restoration intended to increase the house's 'period charm' rather than from neglect. This volume is aimed at those who wish to look beyond the charm, and to see in wood and stone evidence of the struggles, pretensions and achievements of generations of our ancestors.

The book is not intended as a catalogue of buildings of historical interest in the county, but rather it aims to describe how the homes of Oxfordshire people have changed over the centuries, and how prevailing social conditions, fashions and building technology have produced those changes. Examples

Timber, brick, thatch and tile blend harmoniously in these cottages at Aston Tirrold in the 1930s

taken from many thousands of buildings and from all parts of the county are used to illustrate the story, with the help of old and new photographs, engravings and plans. It is not useful here to draw a firm distinction between the 'vernacular' traditions of the village craftsman and the 'polite' architecture produced for the local manor house. Oxfordshire was never remote from the latest developments in architectural practice and we shall see how the new ideas of each generation filtered down the social scale, from the great country houses to the houses of the yeoman farmer and the agricultural labourer.

Children pose outside a stone and thatch cottage in Hinton Waldrist early in the twentieth century. Road traffic was apparently no hazard

Oxfordshire is a particularly interesting county to study. For most of its history it has been a relatively prosperous region able to afford well-built housing, and yet it has largely escaped the virtual rebuilding experienced by many counties more closely associated with the Industrial Revolution. It has always been a rural county, but nevertheless its prosperity was not entirely derived from tilling the soil: the Cotswold wool trade financed fine merchants' houses in Burford, domestic crafts such as gloving and lace-making brought money into villages such as Woodstock and Charlbury, and, of course, the University and a relative proximity to London attracted men of national wealth and prestige into the county.

Oxfordshire's houses are particularly interesting for other reasons too. Before the railways brought cheap transport for mass-produced building materials, builders had to make the best use of whatever was available locally, and in this area that could be very diverse. In the Middle Ages only the wealthy could afford to use anything other than timber, earth and thatch, but from the sixteenth century onwards an increasing prosperity enabled those close to suitable stone to build in a more permanent way. In the north of the county this meant using the tawny-brown ironstone, while in the Cotswold area the fine honey-coloured limestone was found to be eminently suitable for both walls and roofs. In the Chiltern hills to the east, use was made of the local hard flintstone, and later many areas found that they had suitable clay for brick-making on their doorsteps. In other words, we shall see how craftsmen have used materials around them to their best advantage and in so doing have given each part of the county its own individual identity.

1 Houses of the Medieval Period

Our knowledge of Oxfordshire's medieval buildings is a very partial one. Until recent times most secular buildings were constructed of materials that were expected to survive no more than a generation or two, and only the wealthy could afford to build in more permanent materials. We can only guess at the appearance of the flimsy dwellings of the great majority of the population, although archaeologists have recently added greatly to our understanding. Walking over the site of a village abandoned after the Black Death can give us a good impression of the tiny size of most of the cottages whose outlines are still discernable as grassy platforms containing the remains of numerous rebuildings, one upon the other. Tusmore, near Cottisford, is such a village in this area, now grazed by sheep.

Fortunately for us, many of the barons and knights of medieval Oxfordshire did choose to build in stone, and we shall presently look at some of their houses that have survived. However, to understand the medieval house, whether large or small, we must first envisage a very communal lifestyle with little of the privacy or personal space that we now regard as essential. Society was organized on the basis of ties of personal loyalty, whether feudal or family, and this was often focused on the hearth around which much of daily life took place. For the humble villein a one-roomed house often had to suffice, or at best two rooms, one of them containing the hearth and the other an unheated sleeping space. For the lord of the manor the great hall was at the core of his house because it contained the hearth, which was a symbol of protection and hospitality, and around it his family, household and guests would eat, be entertained and sometimes sleep. Indeed, to feed lavishly a large household and numerous guests was regarded as essential to the prestige of a great man. We can imagine the noisy and smoky atmosphere in the hall on a winter's evening, the lord and his family eating at a table placed on a dais at the top of the hall and his dependants eating at long tables placed down either side with a roaring fire on a hearth in the centre. Often this 'extended family' would be entertained by musicians or singers, and many of the remains of the meal would lie scattered on the straw-strewn floor. The hall was open to the rafters and the smoke from the fire was expected to find its own way out through the thatch or through a small louvre in the roof, but no doubt much of it hung heavily over the diners. To lessen this nuisance halls were often built very high, lit by tall windows, and the bare expanses of wall were usually painted or hung with expensive tapestries. The tapestries were both decorative and served the practical function of absorbing some of the echoes of large stone rooms, and they were often carried from house to house with the other household valuables when the lord and his retinue moved. Only gradually did the lord's family come to demand private rooms for their own use, starting with the first-floor great chamber, or solar, so called because it was placed on the first floor (from Old French *sol*, meaning floor), and this was usually directly accessible by a stair from the dais of the hall. This chamber became the family's private bed-sitting room, although even this was usually shared with the personal servants and real privacy was only to be found within the four-poster bed. But despite the addition of the chamber, and later of a parlour and further chambers, the communal hall was to remain at the heart of the English house until the sixteenth century.

Sadly we can no longer see the great palaces where many of the kings of medieval England held their splendid courts: Woodstock was demolished in the eighteenth century to make way for Blenheim, and Beaumont Palace, where Richard I was born, once stood on the site of the present Beaumont Street in Oxford. However, Broughton Castle near Banbury was one of the great medieval houses of the county and much of it has survived as the core of the present, largely sixteenth-century house. It was built for Sir John de Broughton, a Knight of

Sometimes louvres were provided in the roofs of medieval halls to let out the smoke from the central hearth. This house in Old Woodstock was given something far superior: a chimney hollowed out from a single block of stone

Edward I who served abroad and against the Scots, and architectural evidence suggests that the main part of the building was completed before his death in 1315. The house was fortified and protected by a moat, though it was designed primarily for comfort rather than defence. The visitor can still see Sir John's great hall which retains many of its original features, despite having been remodelled in the sixteenth century when the plaster ceiling was inserted and the tall, traceried windows replaced. At the west end the original position of three small doorways can be seen: the central one would have given access to the kitchen, most likely detached and placed away from the main buildings because of the risk of fire, and the small pointed arches to either side were the entrances to the buttery and pantry. The buttery, closely guarded by the butler, was for the storage of wine and beer, and the pantry was for food. Directly in front of these doors, and within the hall, would have been the screens passage with exterior doors at each end. The idea of the screen was to contain the draughts from the doors. It probably originated as a curtain but later developed into a wooden partition placed across the width of the hall with a central door. The screen was often decorated with fine carvings in the larger houses, and access was sometimes given to its roof to create a minstrels' gallery, as was the case at Broughton. Traditionally the hall side of the house was referred to as being 'above' the passage and the service side as being 'below', and it is possible to gain a good impression of the medieval arrangement from the halls of many Oxford and Cambridge colleges where screens passages can still be seen fulfilling their original functions. At the other end of the hall would have been a raised dais for the high table, and a narrow spiral staircase in the corner at Broughton still leads to Sir John's solar, raised over a finely vaulted undercroft and lit by one of the original windows.

Another of the great houses of medieval Oxfordshire is Minster Lovell Hall on the banks of the Windrush near Witney. Unlike Broughton it later fell into decay and the visitor today sees a splendid ruin cared for by English Heritage, uncluttered by later additions. Although the manor belonged to the Lovell family from the twelfth century, the present building is the work of William, seventh Lord Lovell, and dates from the early decades of the fifteenth century. We know that Lord Lovell was serving in the French Wars until 1431 and that in 1440 he obtained a royal licence to 'impark a parcel of land called

The great hall of Minster Lovell Hall, near Witney, built in the early fifteenth century. It is now cared for by English Heritage

"Mintstrewodes", with two fields adjacent to the woods belonging to his manor of Minstrelovell'. We may surmise that construction of the house was also taking place at this time. The building as it stands today is constructed on a courtyard plan around a huge courtyard, with the great hall, chapel and solar forming the main block, and further accommodation, kitchens, a bakehouse and stables being ranged in two long wings reaching down to the Windrush, which forms the fourth side of the quadrangle. As at Broughton, the hall is the focus of the plan, but this one must have outshone all others in the county for it measures fifteen metres long and twelve metres high, and was lit by large traceried windows that once contained a series of heraldic medallions in stained glass. There are no fireplaces in the hall so it must have been heated by a central hearth, and three openings in one of the gables suggest that some form of ventilation was provided. The entrance to the screens passage was through an exceptionally fine, vaulted porch on the north side, and the door at the other end of the passage opened into the courtyard. At the opposite end of the hall stood the dais for the lord's table, and behind it were two doors: one would have led to the chapel and the other to a spiral stair to the solar, Lord Lovell's principal private apartment. This was a comfortable room lit by a large two-light traceried window and heated by a fireplace, part of which survives, surmounted by a tall hexagonal chimney. We should, of course, imagine these rooms alive with the sounds of a large number of residents, including not only the lord's household but also retainers, visitors and manorial officials, for this was not a rural retreat but rather the

The detached kitchen of Stanton Harcourt Manor House probably dates from the late fourteenth century (Engraving by Parker, 1859)

administrative and judicial headquarters of a powerful man. There would have been bailiffs from distant estates bringing in rents and dues, tenants coming with petitions and grievances, lawyers attending to important cases and, of course, numerous knights and companions crowding into these rooms and courtyards. Life was, however, risky for a great man in the turbulent politics of the fifteenth century, and the eighth Lord Lovell's support for the Yorkist side in the Wars of the Roses was the cause of his downfall and the seizure of the estate by the Crown.

Unfortunately little remains of the large medieval house at Stanton Harcourt to the west of Oxford except for its detached kitchen. Most of the house was demolished in 1750 when the Harcourt family seat was moved to Nuneham, but the kitchen

Norman Hall, Sutton Courtenay, is a remarkable survival. It was probably built in about 1191 by Robert de Courtenay and has a finely ornamented doorway

alone is well worth a visit because it is one of the best surviving examples of its kind in Britain. Kitchens built on a grand scale were regarded as essential symbols of aristocratic prestige in the same way as dining halls. This one is square in plan and measures about ten metres on each face. It was probably part of Thomas Harcourt's late fourteenth-century house and it has been little altered since, except for the replacement of the roof in 1485. On entering the dark interior it is not difficult to imagine teams of cooks roasting meat on spits over the two huge fires that were ranged against one wall, or baking bread in the ovens on the opposite wall. The exceptional height of the building was designed to take the resulting smoke and heat, for there were no chimneys but only wide openings under the octagonal pyramid roof. The poet Alexander Pope, who lodged with the family between 1717 and 1718, was amazed to find this immense kitchen still in regular use and wrote that, 'by the blackness of the walls, the circular fires, vast cauldrons, yawning mouths of ovens and furnaces, you would think it . . . the forge of Vulcan'.

Of course these magnificent piles were not typical of the homes of the many knights and manorial lords of medieval Oxfordshire. In the years after the Conquest buildings other than churches were rarely constructed in stone, but the small Norman Hall in Sutton Courtenay is a remarkable exception. It is a compact rectangular building, and it still retains some of its

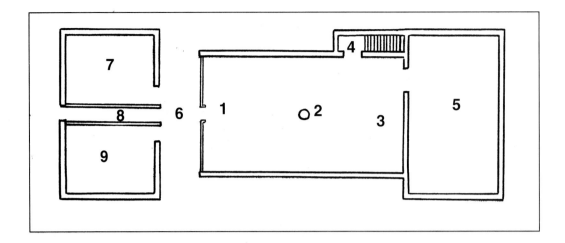

Plan of a typical medieval hall house. 1 hall, 2 hearth, 3 dais, 4 stair to solar, 5 solar (above), 6 screens passage, 7 buttery, 8 passage to detached kitchen, 9 pantry

seven lancet windows and original south doorway ornamented with shafts, roll mouldings and dog-tooth decoration similar to that around the doors of Norman churches. It was probably built by Robert de Courtenay soon after 1191 when he paid the king 300 marks to 'enjoy' the manor of Sutton, and he made it the finest house in the area. It is unusual for stone houses of this period in having its hall on the ground floor rather than on the first, which would have provided extra security from attack. Timber buildings were always at risk from fire, so such a precaution would have been useless, but in this case the ground-floor hall probably indicates that Robert felt himself under no threat from his neighbours.

Few builders could afford impressive courtyard houses, but the more compact H-plan of a single-storey hall flanked by two-storey cross wings was widely adopted for the smaller medieval houses of the county. It contained all the elements essential for medieval living: a central hall open to the rafters, an upstairs solar in the wing at the dais end of the hall, and a pantry, kitchen and buttery, with a chamber for sleeping above, in the wing at the other end. At Charney Bassett in the south-west of the county Abingdon Abbey, the owners of the manor, built a house in stone for their own use, and although the hall and north wing have been replaced by nineteenth-century structures, the south wing stands little changed since it was completed in about 1280. This wing accommodated the chapel and solar over an undercroft, and it has a fine crown-post roof where the rafters are supported by vertical crown posts placed in the centre of the roof and standing on tie-beams. The three-bay solar measures some nine metres by

The 'Abbey' in Sutton Courtenay was built by the monks of Abingdon Abbey and has parts that date back to about 1330

five metres, and has a two-light window with stone seats in the embrasures and rebates for the wooden shutters, which would originally have kept out the elements before the addition of glazing. On the south wall there is evidence of a blocked doorway that would have led to a staircase or garderobe, and a door on the east wall leads into a small chapel which no doubt would have been used by the monks as a private oratory.

A little later in date, but also built by the monks of Abingdon Abbey, is the rectory or 'Abbey' in Sutton Courtenay, and here the original hall still stands open to the rafters behind a later frontage. Despite this being a relatively small building, the hall measures some twelve metres by seven metres and would have accommodated a large number of diners. Its grandeur is heightened by a splendid timber roof supported by a crown post with four angled struts, which stand on a huge moulded truss resting on carved corbels protruding from the walls. This roof was clearly intended to be decorative as well as functional, and mouldings on the hoods over the doorways to the screens passage confirm a date of construction of about 1330. As at Broughton and Minster Lovell, the open hall would have been at the core of the house, both physically and in its part in daily life. Here we should imagine not the splendour of a great court but rather a few practical furnishings, such as trestle tables that could be folded away after the meal, long benches and perhaps a boarded chest in which to lock away plate or expensive clothes. After the meal the monks could retire to a solar lit by a large traceried window, which could be reached from the

An unusual fourteenth-century timber roof over the hall in the 'Abbey', Sutton Courtenay (Engraving by Parker, 1853)

dais end of the hall. This was clearly a comfortable benefice and it attracted several eminent incumbents including Robert de Walsham (1372–84), chaplain to the Black Prince.

A stone-built house would have been a large investment for a small landowner and, rather than demolish it, subsequent generations would often merely make their own additions or modifications to suit changing needs. Sometimes new wings were built around an old core: in the case of the Manor House in Sutton Courtenay, the vaulted cellar of an eleventh-century building was incorporated into a late fourteenth-century house with an open hall, and this in turn became the core of a largely sixteenth-century house. More often, however, the original parts were altered beyond recognition and architectural historians have to piece together clues to understand the house's history.

The pointed doorway and blocked window of the Leadenporch House, Deddington, are the only exterior clues to the fourteenth-century origins of this house

The Leadenporch House in the High Street in Deddington, for example, appears at first sight to be a typical two-storey seventeenth-century house built in the red ironstone that is characteristic of the northern part of the county. The tall, pointed doorway facing the street and a traceried window, now blocked, seem perplexing and out of context, but a visit to the attic reveals that this house has a long and interesting history. Instead of a seventeenth-century roof there are massive timbers of an early fourteenth-century construction, encrusted with centuries of soot from the fire of a room open to the rafters. This was clearly once the hall of a medieval yeoman farmer or merchant who was keen to copy, on a small scale, the lifestyle of the great lords of the day, and the large window with its transom and traceried head, together with the stout roof, must have added style to a relatively modest hall. Subsequently the house was completely remodelled with new rooms upstairs, several new mullioned windows and a large fireplace inserted in front of the original window, but the family was obviously happy to retain parts of the house of its ancestors.

The great majority of houses built before the sixteenth century were of timber. In the south and east of the county the cost of transporting stone would have been prohibitive, and even where good stone was readily available the high cost of dressing and handling it would have put it beyond the reach of most householders. Consequently we should picture villages

Yelford Manor is a remarkable example of a fifteenth-century timber-framed manor house. It is pictured here in the 1920s, before the exterior plaster was removed

throughout Oxfordshire built almost exclusively of timber and thatch, even in the Cotswolds and other parts of the county that we now associate with the stone tradition. Most timber buildings were of poor construction and have not survived, but in recent decades architectural historians have shown that a surprising quantity of medieval timberwork can still be found, often contained within much altered buildings. The better quality houses were constructed by the box-frame technique, whereby long, straight timbers were assembled on the ground and then erected and tenoned together. This was suitable for large buildings, including those of one or more storeys where the upper floors overhang those beneath, a form of construction known as a 'jetty'. This technique, which could be repeated on several floors, provided extra space upstairs on a constricted town site and also, and perhaps more importantly, avoided the necessity of joining the upper and lower wall posts with the horizontal floor joists all at the same point. The overhang could be on more than one side, and in this case a massive corner post was inserted, usually an upturned tree-trunk.

Even large manor houses were sometimes constructed of timber, and Yelford Manor near Bampton is a remarkable example of a fifteenth-century box-frame house that has been changed little over the centuries. It was built for the Hastings family on an H-plan on a moated site next to the church, and a

Market day, Thame, in the late nineteenth century. Medieval towns acted as vital market centres for their agricultural hinterlands

large hall, originally with a central hearth, still occupies the centre of the building. At one end of the hall stood the lord's dais, its original position being visible externally by a hexagonal bay window that served to light it, and at the other end would have been the screens passage with exterior doors at each end. Short two-storey cross wings stand at each end of the hall, the one beyond the screens passage accommodating the buttery, kitchen and pantry, and that next to the dais end of the hall the lord's solar and chambers. The recent removal of the exterior plaster has revealed the close-studded timberwork, a form of high-quality carpentry popular in the fifteenth century in which the vertical posts were set close together with a minimum of infilling. Unfortunately we know little of the original interior decoration but some surviving traces of red and gold stripes point to a once lavish design of the highest quality.

The towns of this period were also constructed almost exclusively of timber, but few town houses have escaped the ravages of time and fire. Most of Oxfordshire's inhabitants of the fifteenth century gained their livelihood through the manorial system of husbandry, but towns such as Oxford, Banbury and Abingdon acted as vital market centres for their surrounding regions, and, of course, Oxford also supplied the University with essential goods and services. Many houses were positioned

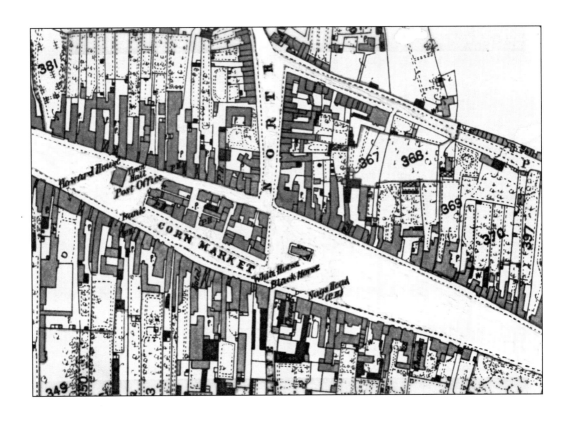

lengthways along the street frontage with spacious vegetable
gardens behind, but in the town centre, and particularly around the
market-place which was the *raison d'etre* of most medieval towns,
they were built with their gables facing the street. This was because
they were set on deep and narrow 'burgage plots' designed to take
up the minimum width of valuable street frontage, and they usually
consisted of a shop at the front and the hall and chambers behind,
with a small garden at the back where refuse could be buried. They
could be one or two rooms wide, and three or four storeys high,
and their position can sometimes be inferred from aerial
photographs or Ordnance Survey maps because the long, narrow
shapes of the burgage plots have often been perpetuated into
modern property boundaries. Then, as now, town properties were
frequently erected by wealthy landlords as commercial ventures,
and an early example of such a venture in Oxford is the former
Tackley's Inn in the High Street. This building, now much altered,
was constructed in the early years of the fourteenth century by the
rector of Tackley as a hall house intended for rent.

It is hard now to imagine the appearance of a medieval town

The fourteenth-century
Birdcage Inn, Thame.
(Isometric drawing)

with its narrow streets and timber houses huddled cheek-by-jowl, but a few of the better-quality buildings have survived in Oxfordshire, including the remarkable Bird Cage Inn in Thame. Standing in the middle of the Market Place, this three-storey building probably originally served as a shop, or shops, with accommodation above for the merchant, but it is possible that it may have been built as a market hall with open sides on the ground floor. Either way, it is a good town building of the fourteenth century, built high to take maximum advantage of a small site and with double jetties on three sides. The heavy

A fourteenth-century house, shop and former inn on the corner of Cornmarket Street and Ship Street, Oxford

timbers are typical of framing of this early date, and the quality of its construction is emphasized by the rich roll mouldings on the massive corner posts at ground-floor level. In the fifteenth century elaborate oriel windows were inserted on the first floor and two of these have survived on the west elevation.

Oxford has nothing to compare with the Bird Cage, but recent work of restoration and partial reconstruction has brought to notice a late fourteenth-century timber building on the corner of Cornmarket Street and Ship Street. The work, undertaken by the owners, Jesus College, with a grant from English Heritage, involved dismantling and re-erecting much of the structure in order to understand its history and restore it as accurately as possible. As it now stands the building in fact incorporates parts of three medieval structures: two houses with shops below facing Cornmarket Street, and an inn behind on Ship Street, of which a first-floor hall and part of a jettied gallery around the courtyard survive. The Cornmarket façade is of three storeys, with jetties to the first and second floors and three steep gables, and it has been restored on evidence from the surviving timbers and nineteenth-century drawings.

Burford is a town that we admire today for its Cotswold stone, but in the medieval period it too would have been constructed largely in timber. Little has survived rebuilding, but an exception is the splendid fifteenth-century timber house in the High Street which is now occupied by Messrs W.J. Castle, butchers. It is likely that it

The same building in
Cornmarket Street
(opposite) in the 1930s,
before the recent
restoration

was built for one of the many prosperous merchants of the town
engaged in the wool trade, for Burford was at this time one of the
leading wool markets in the Cotswolds and attracted buyers from as
far afield as Flanders, Florence and Venice. The house is impressive
with its triple gables facing the street, and the high quality of its
carpentry can be seen in the carved bargeboards in the gables. Some
of the original mullioned windows have survived, one of them at the
back of the house having five arched lights. The building may have
been jettied, but this has been hidden by the later expansion of the
shop premises on the ground floor.

Building in the High Street,
Burford, pictured in about
1900. Timber was the
chief building material
even in the Cotswolds in
the fifteenth century

Stone and early brickwork can be seen in the walls of the almshouses in Ewelme, built in the 1430s by the Earl of Suffolk

At the core of any medieval town was a church, and next to the church was often to be found an almshouse provided by a wealthy donor to house the poor and needy of the parish. Abingdon has its Long Alley Almshouses (1446) and Henley its twelve cottages built by John Longland (1530), but by far the most interesting are the almshouses at Ewelme built by William de la Pole, Earl of Suffolk, in the 1430s. Instead of a large communal hall and chapel, as was usual at this time, de la Pole provided thirteen separate dwellings or cells around a central cloister, a plan that echoes that of the Carthusian priories of the period. The exterior walls are of stone, but the chimney-stacks and the infill to the timber-framed interior walls is of brick, making one of the earliest examples of the use of this material in the county. The adjacent schoolhouse was built in brick too and was given two massive chimney-stacks which also serve as buttresses.

Most builders could only afford to use timber, but box-frame construction was itself expensive in both materials and craftsmanship, and many country builders turned to a simpler form of construction: the 'cruck-truss'. By this method curved tree trunks were split longitudinally, erected with their ends meeting at the ridge and then connected at eaves level by a horizontal tie-beam to form an 'A' shape. A house of two or three bays could be erected with a minimum of carpentry by standing three or four trusses at roughly five-metre intervals and joining them by a ridge-beam and horizontal purlins to carry the rafters. The walls could then be filled with light timbers and wattle as they were not required to carry the

The cruck blades are clearly visible in the gable wall of the Barley Mow Inn, Clifton Hampden

weight of the roof, and windows could be placed as desired. This rather primitive method was, of course, only suitable for single-storey buildings, but was widely used in the North of England, the Midlands and Wales up to the fifteenth century, and several examples can be found in Oxfordshire, mostly in the south of the county. The area around Harwell, Steventon and East Hendred is particularly rich in surviving cruck houses. The wide cruck blades can often be seen in the gable of the building, as in the mid-fourteenth-century cottage known as 39 The Causeway, Steventon, and in the Barley Mow inn in Clifton Hampden. Frequently however, because of subsequent refacing in stone, brick or plaster, the cruck construction is not apparent from the exterior and can only be discovered through an interior inspection.

A number of examples have been investigated by architectural historians in Oxfordshire, but the most remarkable must be Orchard End in Waterstock which, though not obvious from its external appearance, is one of the oldest timber buildings in England. The original structure consisted of five cruck trusses, giving the house four bays, of which the central two formed the hall. Most of the medieval timbers are still in place, and the rafters over the central bays, now hidden by modern ceilings, are encrusted with soot. This indicates that the hall had a central hearth, but the sections over the bays at either end of the building show no signs of ever having been exposed to smoke

Orchard End, Waterstock, is a house of cruck construction that may date back to the late thirteenth century

and must always have been partitioned from the hall up to roof level. The partitions divided the heated hall from the unheated parts of the house, which served as the sleeping chambers and store rooms. The feet of the cruck blades are tenoned into cill-beams on rubble footings, but more unusual is the fact that the blades reach only halfway up the roof which is completed by attached rafters, and this probably represents a long-lost local tradition. The dating of these buildings is notoriously difficult, but dendrochronological analysis of the growth rings of the elm timbers suggests a date of erection of around 1295, in the reign of King Edward I.

Cruck houses are the smallest medieval houses to survive but we should not suppose that they are typical of the housing of the peasantry. In fact a house such as that at Waterstock would have required the purchase, transport and cutting of about forty trees, so we can assume that it would have been built for a man of considerable substance in the village.

2 Country Houses of the Tudor Period

The period from the middle of the sixteenth century to the outbreak of the Civil War was one of dramatic economic growth. For the first time after the disastrous ravages of the Black Death, population levels were rising again and indeed in some areas were to double within the century. Many villages expanded and shifted their focus, towns grew, and building in Oxford expanded beyond the medieval walls. As the number of town dwellers multiplied, they demanded increasing quantities of food and country products such as wool and leather, and landowners were soon enjoying the benefits of soaring prices and profits. Some landlords were able to take maximum advantage of rising prices by enclosing the tenanted arable fields in their possession and converting the land to sheep and cattle pasture, thus replacing low rentals by high profits. This often caused considerable hardship and sometimes provoked riots by the dispossessed, as, for example, on the land of Francis Poure of Hampton Gay following his enclosure of ninety-six acres in 1596.

It is not surprising, therefore, that we should see many landlords and squires building on a grand scale during this century. Usually, however, they did not want the old courtyard-plan houses of their predecessors, like Minster Lovell, for they no longer saw themselves as the heads of large households of retainers in these more peaceful days of the Tudor regime. Instead, they wanted to advertise their wealth, education and

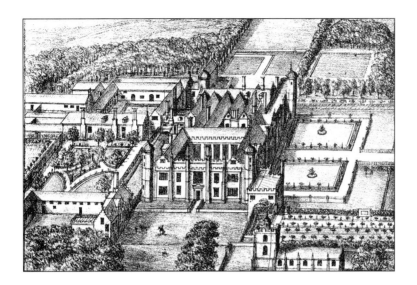

Rycote House, built in the early sixteenth century, was one of the largest in the county until its destruction by fire in 1745. (Engraving by Kip, 1714)

cosmopolitan tastes acquired through contact with court circles, and the result was a ready adoption of highly innovative designs. That is not to say, however, that traditional halls and screen passages were hastily abandoned, for even the most radical of patrons had a nostalgic reverence for the good old days of chivalry and hospitality, and the mixture of the old and the new often produced some rather bizarre results.

Rycote House, near Thame, was one of the great houses of Oxfordshire when it was built of brick in the early years of the sixteenth century, and it followed a fairly traditional courtyard plan. Sadly the house was burned down in 1745, leaving only a delightful chapel now cared for by English Heritage, and we know little about the house other than what we can deduce from a copperplate print published by Kip in 1714. However, when the owner of Rycote, Sir John Williams, decided to build himself a brand new house at Beckley on the edge of Otmoor, he chose a very different style, and one that was in the vanguard of architectural fashion when it was completed in the 1540s. Fortunately this house still stands surrounded by its moat, and has been little altered since the sixteenth century. It too is constructed not of stone but of plum-coloured bricks, here decorated with darker bricks set in a large diaper pattern and with stone surrounds to the long, mullioned windows. Bricks were not new to the county: records survive of the purchase of 200,000 'brykes' from Crocker End near Nettlebed for Stonor Park in 1417, and, as we

Beckley Park broke new ground with its symmetrical design when it was built in the 1540s, and has been remarkably little altered since

have seen, the Earl of Suffolk had chosen brick for his almshouses and school at Ewelme in 1437. Nevertheless it was the use of brick in the great palaces of Richmond and Hampton Court built for Henry VIII and Cardinal Wolsey that made it a fashionable material, and when Sir John decided to build his lodge at Beckley Park where good-quality stone was not readily available, he could afford to select the very latest style in brick.

Beckley Park breaks with tradition in more important ways, however. Instead of the rambling irregularity of medieval courtyards this house consists of just one compact block, and its façade is symmetrical with a central entrance porch and regular rows of windows on either side. The influence here came from the classical Renaissance which was developed firstly in Italy, where Roman ruins and styles had always been familiar, and was then taken up in France, the Netherlands and England. Builders of this period were more interested in grafting classical details onto basically medieval buildings than in trying to capture the essence of the classical style, but the Renaissance concern for symmetry and proportion struck a particular chord with sixteenth-century thought, and many cultured patrons insisted that this should be reflected in their buildings as in other spheres of life. At the same time they were reluctant to dispense with the traditional room arrangement of the hall, with an off-centre screens passage flanked by a parlour on one side and the buttery and kitchens on the other, which was convenient but not symmetrical. Architects were to wrestle for another century with

Broughton Castle, near Banbury, was 'modernized' in the late sixteenth century by the Fiennes family (Print by Buck, 1729)

the problem of how to unite a symmetrical façade with a medieval room plan, but at Beckley a rather ungainly expedient was resorted to: an extra window to light the buttery was required to the right of the door and, so as not to disturb the symmetry of the main windows, a tiny triangular window was inserted abutting onto the porch so as to be as inconspicuous as possible. Yet although the traditional plan was retained, the hall was built only one-storey high with rooms above it instead of being open to the height of the house, and this reflects its declining status in the sixteenth-century house.

It appears that Lord Williams's ideas on sanitation were as developed as those on design, for at the back of the house three unusual gabled towers rise to the height of the house, the central one to accommodate a staircase and the other two to act as the shafts for privies located on the top floor. One wonders whether this arrangement was as satisfactory in practice as it appeared on paper, but it certainly demonstrates the willingness of the Tudor architect to experiment with highly individual designs.

Richard Fiennes of Broughton Castle, near Banbury, no doubt looked on in dismay as the glory of his medieval house became tarnished in comparison with the more up-to-date designs of some of his neighbours, and in the 1550s he decided on a radical remodelling. The medieval hall was retained but the entrance front was given a face lift: it was increased in height to give it extra grandeur, the irregular gothic windows were replaced by symmetrical mullioned windows like those at Beckley, and two square bays with huge windows were added, one of which served to hide the off-centre entrance to the screens passage. As the façade lacked a central focus, Fiennes added a projecting first-floor oriel window decorated with fashionable Ionic and Corinthian columns, thus strangely uniting an essentially gothic window with classical detail.

However, the most stunning transformations were those made to the interior of the house. They were started in 1554 and completed by Richard Fiennes the Younger in the 1590s, and they produced some of the finest rooms in the county of this date. The first priority was to reduce the dominance of the hall by the insertion of a plaster ceiling and the creation of a number of smaller rooms above it. One of these was fitted with a magnificent stucco fireplace, carved with female figures supporting a large oval cartouche depicting a scene from Ovid's *Metamorphoses*. This was very advanced for its date and was possibly inspired by similar work at Henry VIII's palace at Nonsuch, since destroyed. The house was then extended by the construction of a new kitchen at the end of the old solar block, and the conversion of the former kitchens into two opulently decorated rooms with large mullioned windows and plasterwork ceilings. One of these, originally the dining room, has oak panelling with geometric panels articulated by giant fluted pilasters, and incorporates a splendid and very unusual interior porch carved with pilasters, cartouches and strapwork designs. This combination of classical motifs and flamboyant strapwork is typical of the Renaissance taste of this period, which was absorbed through France and Flanders and picked up many local influences on the way.

Broughton Castle of the 1590s was therefore a very different house to that of Sir John de Broughton in the fourteenth century. The hall is now much reduced in status and is no longer the focus of daily living, the formal splendour and etiquette of baronial eating having been replaced by the privacy of meals taken largely in the comfort of much smaller rooms which were opulently decorated and furnished. Almost all the structural fabric of the building had now been hidden: the walls with oak panelling, the ceiling beams with fine plasterwork and the fireplace surrounded by a carved chimney-piece and overmantel. Family life had withdrawn from the very public great hall firstly to the chamber, and then to a series of parlours and withdrawing rooms to which guests were invited according to their intimacy and importance.

The cosy comfort of the sixteenth-century parlour can be seen nowhere better than in Thame Park, a house that incorporates the abbot's lodgings of a Cistercian abbey. The parlour of the lodging was added by Robert King, the last abbot who resided

Thame Park incorporates
the abbot's lodging of a
Cistercian abbey dissolved
by Henry VIII

This parlour at Thame
Park was decorated in the
1530s in the most lavish
style by the last abbot

The façade of Burford
Priory before it was
drastically remodelled.
This impressive house was
built by Sir Lawrence
Tanfield in the late
sixteenth century (Print by
Skelton)

there before its dissolution in 1539, and he decorated it in the latest and most sumptuous style. The room is heated by a broad fireplace, and draughts from the door are contained by an internal porch similar to that at Broughton. Above the linenfold panelling, the walls and ceiling are covered in brightly painted Renaissance decorations within carved panels, and, though they are now rather faded, we can imagine how comfortable and fashionable the room must have looked to contemporary eyes.

We have looked at the new comforts being enjoyed by the great landlords, but they were not the only ones to benefit from the new Tudor age. The gradual replacement of the rule of force by the rule of law created a new class of civil servants and lawyers, many of whom were quick to invest their wealth in land and houses, and some were able to purchase ex-monastic property sold after the Dissolution. Sir Lawrence Tanfield is a good example of such a man. He was an eminent lawyer and Lord Chief Baron of the Exchequer under Queen Elizabeth, and he purchased the remains of Burford Priory in 1580 to build a

Chastleton House is a tall, square house built for Witney wool merchant, Walter Jones, in the early years of the seventeenth century

grand new house on the site which was once one of the most important houses of the county. Although it has since been altered and reduced in size out of all recognition, its original form is shown in an engraving by Skelton published in 1808. The house was built on an E-plan with a central porch and wings at each end, the porch being intended to stress the symmetry of the façade around a central entrance, and it was given three storeys with attics and five gables to make the maximum impression on arrival. It was also a comfortable house with large mullioned windows filled with expensive glass, and numerous fireplaces which were advertised by a forest of chimneys on the skyline.

The Tudor age also heralded a rapid growth in trade and commerce, both internal and foreign, and some of the most innovative houses were built by successful merchants and financiers who were keen to impress the established landowners of the county. Witney wool merchant Walter Jones was no exception, and in 1602 he commissioned a leading architect, probably Robert Smythson, to design Chastleton House on a hilltop near the present western edge of the county. This house now stands remarkable not only for its design, but also for its state of preservation, and these factors were uppermost in the mind of the National Trust when it purchased the house in 1991.

The main doorway at Chastleton House is embellished by strapwork and classical designs

Jones's requirements were typical of his day, for he wanted stunning grandeur rather than rambling accommodation for retainers, and thus the house is square, compact and tall. The impression of height is reinforced by the vertical emphasis of a series of projecting bays and towers, which lead the eye up to the narrow gables and numerous chimneys on the skyline. Smythson is well known for his 'glass palaces' of Hardwick Hall and Wollaton, and Chastleton too was given large, mullioned and transomed windows filled with expensive glass. As at Beckley and Broughton, the hall is relatively small in relation to the house, and the emphasis is instead on lavishly decorated private rooms. Nevertheless, Jones was reluctant to break with tradition entirely, so the hall is still at the centre of the ground floor, and the symmetry of the façade is here maintained by putting the entrance to the off-centre screens passage in the side wall of one of the projecting bays, making it virtually invisible from the front.

At the back of the house on the top floor runs the long gallery, that most appealing of Elizabethan innovations. Here money was lavished on a vaulted ceiling decorated with rich plasterwork and oak panelling below with a frieze of acorns. Galleries were placed on the top floor of large houses for the views of the surrounding countryside and were originally conceived as a pleasant place to exercise in bad weather or to walk with guests. They soon became an important room in the house, and their walls were often hung with portraits of the family and of various worthies, both alive and dead, which were intended to inspire the viewer and shed reflected glory onto the family.

The interior decoration of Chastleton is an example of Flemish Renaissance pattern-book designs at their most exuberant. The hall screen is carved with acanthus scrolls, satyrs and half-columns, and the great chamber on the first floor is fitted with panelling smothered with fluted pilasters, blind arcading and Flemish strapwork, above which is a fine plaster ceiling. The result is a heavy sense of opulence which is often classical in its detail but most unclassical in its effect.

The Tudor and Jacobean country house stands at a crossroads between the medieval and the classical house, and often expresses a feeling of vitality and experimentation that we find so attractive today. The innovations in lifestyle and comfort made in these houses were soon taken up by builders of more

Kelmscott Manor, near
Faringdon, dates from
about 1570 and is now
well known for its
associations with the
nineteenth-century
designer, William Morris

modest means, including the local gentry, and Oxfordshire
possesses many examples of manor houses in a style taken
directly from the great Elizabethan houses. Kelmscott Manor,
near Faringdon, for example, is a stone-built house of about
1570. Though relatively small in size, it is equipped with large,
glazed and mullioned windows and numerous fireplaces. The
ground plan is still very traditional with a hall divided from the
kitchen by a screens passage, but the exterior is given dignity by
its height and the tall gables on all sides, and the stonework is
finely finished in the Cotswold tradition. Shipton Court in
Shipton-under-Wychwood is a much larger house on an H-plan
built in the early seventeenth century, but it follows a similar
style with narrow gables topped by finials and well-proportioned
mullioned windows.

This was however the end of an age, for within half a century
all of these houses were to appear very old-fashioned in their
broken façades and flamboyant skylines, for a new broom was
soon to sweep through architecture with frightening speed. We
shall see the effects on Oxfordshire in Chapter 4.

3   The Great Rebuilding

The second half of the sixteenth century and first half of the seventeenth are often referred to as the period of the Great Rebuilding, not only because they produced a number of innovative houses built for the nobility, gentry and rising merchant classes, but also because, for the first time, the small yeoman farmers and husbandmen were reconstructing their houses in more durable materials. As the price of agricultural products rose, many smaller producers were in a good position to increase their output by improving their farming practices, for example by cooperating to enclose the old open fields. Yeoman farmers were thus able to accumulate money to buy out their neighbours and thus build up substantial farms. Legal records show that more land changed hands between 1540 and 1570 than in any period since the Conquest, and many of these transactions were

The Causeway in the 1920s. Steventon is rich in such Elizabethan timber-framed houses

Much old timberwork lies hidden by later façades in Harwell. This fourteenth-century roof survives in the upper rooms of King's Manor

between yeoman farmers. Even tenant copyholders were often finding their fixed rent less onerous as their income rose, especially when they were largely self-sufficient for food.

Prosperous farmers were also investing their surplus income in houses to introduce some comfort and privacy into their lives and to proclaim their rising social status and pretensions. William Harrison, in his *Description of England* published in 1577, wrote that people were enjoying more comfort in their homes, stone was replacing timber in many areas, glazed windows were now commonplace, and, most significantly, he wondered at 'the multitude of chimneys lately erected'. Of course, different parts of the county experienced this rebuilding at different dates, for while the lowland areas to the east were able to profit fairly early from the buoyant demand for food from London, many of the distinctive stone-built villages of the upland Cotswolds were the result of rebuilding in the seventeenth century.

The rising standards of living enjoyed by the smaller farmer can be graphically illustrated by the numerous wills and inventories made in the years after the Reformation, many of which survive in the Oxfordshire Archives. The inventories of the goods left by the deceased often provide us with a room-by-room description of the houses of this period. Take, for example, the inventory of the goods of John Sims of Dorchester-on-Thames made on 16 May 1553. Sims farmed fifty-five acres of

A row of jettied, timber-framed town houses in Friday Street, Henley-on-Thames, in about 1887

arable land and yet it appears that his family lived in a one-roomed house, which must have been open to the rafters as the list includes '3 hogges in the roof', presumably as bacon curing over the smoky fire. His furniture comprised little more than 'one cobbord . . . a forme, a table and stolles'. By contrast, the inventory of Richard Collins of Wolvercote, taken some thirty-four years later, lists the comfortable contents of a ten-roomed house, although Collins was farming only thirty-five acres. In his hall he had a 'cubbarde, a joined table, a foorme [and] foure chaires', while his parlour contained 'five coffers, a setle, a forme [and] a joined bedsteede' with a 'painted tester', this clearly being his private bed-sitting room. Other rooms in the house included the kitchen, well equipped with 'seven pottes, eight ketles, three Pannes' and other utensils, the buttery and a chamber over the hall furnished with 'a litle Cubbard . . . A Cheeste [and] a Table'. Collins was clearly living a very different lifestyle to John Sims, and the reference to a room over the hall indicates that the hall cannot have been open to the rafters and must therefore have been equipped with a chimney-stack. Nor was Richard Collins unique. Looking through the inventories of Harwell, for example, we can find nine or ten yeoman families who left new houses of five or more rooms in the late sixteenth century, in a town where the population increased from about 200 in 1525 to about 350 in 1660. We can read of men such as John Jennings who died in 1599 leaving goods worth £273, including a newly built house, to his wife and ten or eleven children. This was a golden age

Wickens Stores, East Hendred, was built in about 1500. It is timber-framed with brick infilling and consists of a hall and two cross wings

for the yeoman farmer, when his status and wealth relative to the great landowners was better than ever before – and, indeed, better than it was to be again.

The rebuilding of modest houses in more permanent materials brought about a divergence in the building traditions of different parts of the county. In the south and east, good-quality timberwork was used in houses much lower down the social scale than had been the case previously, but in the north and west timber-framing was largely replaced by locally quarried stone. In part this was the result of rising prosperity, but in addition the price of good-quality timber rose as local woodlands diminished. John Leland noted in his *Itinerary in England and Wales* that Haseley was 'baren of wood as al that angle of Oxfordshir is'. Sometimes use had to be made of alternatives to stone, such as soft chalk and cob in the Vale and flint nodules in the Chilterns.

Around Oxford and towards Witney, limestone rubble was available, and although it was not suitable for cutting, it could be laid in courses. The Old Manor House at Poffley End, Hailey, is an example of the developments that were taking place in the early sixteenth century in this area. The house was constructed of rubble stone in the early decades of the century as a two-storey open hall with a kitchen at one end, a solar over it and a storeroom behind. Later in the century the occupant, possibly a Robert Yate, transformed the house with many of the

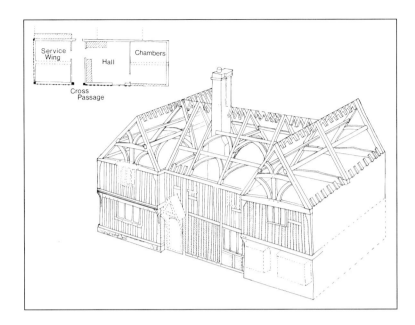

Wickens Stores, East Hendred (Isometric drawing)

improvements that characterize the period. A chimney-stack was inserted into the hall, with a spiral stair beside it leading to new chambers on the first floor which had been created over the hall. The kitchen was made into the living room, also heated by the central chimney, and the store was converted into a new kitchen with its own chimney. The result of this work was to reduce the hall to just another sitting room, to expand the number of rooms to create more space and privacy, and to make life more comfortable through the provision of fireplaces and of glazing in the windows.

Stone was not available in the south of the county, so here builders had no choice but to continue to use timber. Wickens Stores in East Hendred is typical of the houses of the lesser gentry of this period. It was built in about 1500 as a three-bay timber-framed house comprising a single-storey open hall with a screens passage, and cross wings at each end with projecting jetties at the front. At some point in the sixteenth century a central chimney-stack was inserted and upstairs rooms were created over the hall, but otherwise it remained largely unchanged until the shop-front was added much later. The construction is of box-frame type with close-studded timberwork. Particularly interesting is that the infilling is not of wattle and daub as one might have expected but of brick 'nogging' set in a herringbone pattern, and it appears that this is original to the

Elizabethan timber houses, Long Wittenham, in about 1900

house. Clearly this was a transitional stage between timber and brick, and the builder in this case purchased expensive bricks to improve a traditional type of construction rather than to replace it.

It could be argued that the introduction of the chimney to modest houses represents the greatest single advance in living conditions in the sixteenth century. It enabled the family to enjoy a number of smaller heated rooms instead of huddling around a central hearth in the hall, bringing the benefits of both comfort and privacy, and it allowed the introduction of better furnishings and painted wall-decoration into a much cleaner house. Chimneys were, however, expensive investments, being best built in brick or dressed stone, and their construction was often undertaken simultaneously with the insertion of an upper storey and other improvements. Documentary evidence of these major changes is rare, but from the farm account books of Robert Loder of Harwell for the years 1610 to 1620 we can read of the expenditure of £6 10s. on 'my chimney ... making my stairs, my window and ceiling and plastering etc'. Because of the high cost of constructing a chimney there was often a desire to make it as large and prominent as possible, almost as a status symbol. Early sixteenth-century brick stacks were often embellished with oversailing courses at the top, and patterns or spirals built into the shafts, while tall, diamond-shaped chimneys became popular in the seventeenth century. The fire-resistant properties of brick

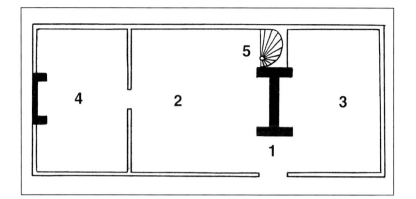

Plan of a lobby–entrance house. 1 entrance lobby, 2 hall, 3 kitchen, 4 parlour, 5 stairs to upper rooms

chimneys were also of interest to the community at a time when fires were a constant hazard, and by the seventeenth century it was often obligatory in many places to build the chimney in brick rather than timber. In Thame, in 1648, a man was presented to court for failing to demolish an old chimney in his house and replace it with one of brick or stone. The fireplaces inside were often as impressive as the chimney-stacks outside, and many were large enough to incorporate bread ovens and seats tucked into an inglenook. It is not unusual to find their surrounds finely carved or moulded in stone, even in modest houses otherwise devoid of ornament, and expensive cast-iron firebacks were purchased for their grates.

When a floor was inserted into the hall the ceiling beams were often given fine mouldings or chamfers with a variety of stops at their ends, and the exact forms used can enable architectural historians to date the work with some degree of precision. Usually the space gained upstairs was only large enough for storage, but sometimes the height of the walls was increased and a new roof constructed to create full-sized bedrooms, thus completely changing the external appearance of the building. Fortunately, many owners merely inserted a ceiling beneath the old roof, leaving the old soot-encrusted beams to be discovered by future generations.

The position chosen for the location of the chimney-stack varied considerably but was usually in accordance with local practice. In the lowland parts of the county a popular position was in the screens passage where it could provide heating for both the hall and the kitchen by placing the fireplaces back-to-back. Of course, this option meant the sacrifice of the screens passage, and on entering the door one is faced by the chimney-

A seventeenth-century lobby-entrance house in Stanton Harcourt. Notice that the central chimney-stack is positioned immediately behind the front door

stack directly in front, thus creating a small lobby with a door to the hall on the left and one to the kitchen on the right. Putting the stack in the passage created the so-called lobby-entrance plan. Fitting in a staircase to the upper rooms was always a problem with this arrangement, but a popular solution was to site a spiral stair (with treads cut from solid blocks of wood) behind the stack where it could be reached from the hall. Unfortunately these have very rarely survived because they were usually replaced by a framed staircase in a different position in the eighteenth or

Fletchers Farm House, Little Milton, is a two-storey seventeenth-century house built on the lobby-entrance plan

The kitchen of Gaunt House, Standlake, in 1901. Notice the large fireplace, and the bacon rack suspended from the ceiling

nineteenth centuries, and it is often difficult to be sure of their original location.

Houses built from the second half of the sixteenth century onwards were given a chimney-stack from new, and were generally of two full storeys with large mullioned and glazed windows. Fletchers Farm House in Little Milton, to the south-east of Oxford, is a good example of a lobby-entrance farmhouse built of stone in the early seventeenth century. It is a neat, rectangular house with a later addition to the rear, and is constructed of limestone rubble with good quality ashlar quoins at the corners, its roof most likely originally being of thatch. At the core of the house is a massive stone stack which separates the parlour from the hall, and a steep stair behind the stack leads to two rooms on the first floor plus a small boxroom over the entrance lobby. Such a building as this would have been typical of the housing of many yeoman farmers of the seventeenth century. It is well built with spacious heated rooms lit by large mullioned and glazed windows, and, although it originally consisted of only four principal rooms, this was a great advance on the housing of the previous century. The hall is now no larger than any of the other rooms and has been merged with the kitchen to create the 'live-in' kitchen so familiar in farmhouses for centuries to come.

Greystone stores, Little Milton, is a stoutly built seventeenth-century farmhouse with its original chimneys

Built to a similar plan, but perhaps more imposing, is Greystone Stores, also in Little Milton. This was once converted into a shop but is now once more a private house. It is still thatched and has the appearance of a very solid and well-built

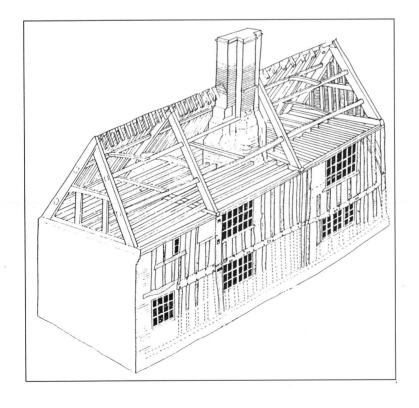

College Cottage, Sparsholt (Isometric drawing)

house, with good-quality masonry and dripstone mouldings over the mullioned windows. It too has a massive brick chimney-stack in the centre of the house, here retaining its diamond-shaped chimneys, and the hall is to the left of the lobby entry and the parlour to the right, with a buttery built on behind.

Timber-framing remained the dominant method of construction in the south of the county throughout the sixteenth and seventeenth centuries – and even into the late eighteenth for humble dwellings. College Cottage in Sparsholt is a three-bay timber-framed house of the mid-sixteenth century, but, unlike Wickens Stores, it was built with a central chimney-stack from new and its rooms were arranged on the lobby-entrance plan: a parlour and kitchen on the ground floor and two bedrooms above. The building is of a full two storeys throughout, without projecting cross wings, and the roof ridge is level along its whole length. Because bricks were still very expensive in this part of the county, the bulk of the chimney-stack is constructed of chalk blocks with only flues projecting above the roof being of brick.

The builder of 55 High Street, Dorchester-on-Thames, had no problem in obtaining adequate supplies of bricks, for he gave his large timber-framed house a huge chimney-stack with four tall, diamond-shaped shafts set on a rectangular base which dominates the façade of the building, and indeed the street. The builder was clearly anxious to show off his wealth and status in the town, and the house, built in 1610, typifies the best-quality timber construction of this period. It never had a single-storey open hall so it was possible to give the building an impressive three storeys, with continuous jetties to both the first and second floors, and no expense was spared in the detail which includes carved scrolled brackets under the jetties. In later years the house was divided into two units and the timber-framing plastered over, but recent work has restored the building to its former glory.

Good-quality timber was, however, becoming an ever scarcer and more expensive commodity, and larger square panels gradually replaced the more profligate close-studded timberwork of previous decades. The width of the timbers also diminished, and wood of a much smaller 'scantling' became commonplace for more modest houses. At the same time the treatment of the timberwork became ever more elaborate with the use of curved

55 High Street, Dorchester-
on-Thames, is a double-
jettied house of 1610 and
has a particularly
impressive chimney-stack

55 High Street, Dorchester-
on-Thames, in the 1920s
before recent restoration

or even serpentine-shaped braces, while the windows became larger and were given moulded mullions and richly carved surrounds. Number 127 The Causeway, Steventon, is a good example of a late sixteenth-century timber house built on an L-shaped plan and consisting of a hall and cross wing, constructed on two storeys from new around a large brick chimney-stack. This house has timbers that are noticeably thin, but the jettied gable proudly displays very decorative framing including turned finials hanging below the jetty, and the room below is well lit by a broad lattice window surrounded by carved woodwork.

The fashion changed quickly in the course of the seventeenth century, and brick and stone came to be regarded as infinitely superior building materials to timber, especially as the quality of available timber declined. Many builders therefore chose to conceal the timber-framing behind a rendering of lime plaster with the intention not only of making a poorer construction more weatherproof, but also of imitating masonry, sometimes even going to the lengths of scoring the plaster to look like the joints in the ashlar. The plaster cladding was then painted white, or colour washed with shades of pink or green, to protect it. As exposed timber-framing came to be seen as vulgar, the owners of houses of high-quality and once fashionable timberwork also chose to apply plaster to the exterior walls to conform to the new taste, and in many cases this has been removed in recent years. The Old Forge in Dorchester-on-Thames was, however, plaster

127 The Causeway, Steventon, is a late sixteenth-century house with broad lattice windows and decorative framing in the gable

The Old Forge, Dorchester-on-Thames, is a lobby-entrance plan house of the seventeenth century. It was probably clad in plaster from new

House in Fawler Road, Uffington, in about 1916, with an outshut extension at the back

clad from new and is a box-frame lobby-entrance house of the seventeenth century. It has a symmetrical façade and a centrally placed brick chimney-stack behind the front door, capped by three diamond-shaped shafts at right angles to the axis of the roof, which heated both ground-floor rooms but only one of the first-floor chambers. Because houses of this period were built to a full two-storey height and have frequently had their original mullioned windows replaced by later sashes, the position and shape of the chimneys is often the best clue to the date of the building. The observer will, of course, also notice that the house is only one-room deep, as were all small houses before the eighteenth century. However, the addition of a single-storey lean-to or 'outshut' at the back of the house to accommodate further service rooms such as a dairy or pantry was a very common expedient.

Anyone motoring around the Cotswolds or the rolling hills around Banbury will be struck by the remarkable homogeneity of both the architecture and the building materials used. This is because many of the houses in these areas were rebuilt in the period 1550 to 1700 when stone replaced timber. Yeoman farmers in these upland areas were particularly prosperous from the raising of sheep in enclosed pastures and from the home manufacture of textiles, and as a consequence the rebuilding here continued to a peak in the middle or late seventeenth century when activity had declined sharply in the lowlands. Here there was little distinction between the yeomanry and the gentry, and their houses were remarkably similar in both style and plan. In the Cotswolds the honey-coloured limestone was easy to carve, and even humble houses were given elaborate gables and finials to the dormers and fine mullions to the windows, but the red ironstone of the north of the county towards Banbury was coarser and found suitable for 'kneelers' at eaves level on the gable ends and for dripstones over the windows. Here thatch remained the dominant roofing material as the stone could not be split into thin slates like the Cotswold limestone.

The yeoman farmers of these relatively isolated hills were intensely proud but conservative men, preferring to 'shape their courses as their fathers did [and] never putting into practice any new device,' as John Norden observed at the end of the sixteenth century. It is perhaps not surprising that many of them were reluctant to insert a chimney-stack into the traditional screens passage, which was no doubt a useful feature in a working farmhouse, and therefore many upland houses chose to retain the passage by siting the chimney-stack in the hall with its back to the screens. The medieval cross-passage plan thus survived to the end of the seventeenth century in these areas, the usual ground plan being to have the kitchen to one side of the passage and the hall and then the parlour to the other, with a spiral stair

A seventeenth-century house in the Cotswold tradition in the High Street, Burford. It has two gables with finials, mullioned windows and a central doorway

Swalcliffe in the 1920s. Red ironstone walls and thatched roofs are characteristic of the northern part of the county

The Mount, Hornton, was built in about 1680 on the cross-passage plan which survived late in the upland regions

between the hall and the parlour to give access to three full-height bedrooms above. Often the house was given three chimney-stacks to give each of the ground-floor rooms its own fireplace. From the middle of the seventeenth century many of the larger houses were also given a cellar under the parlour for the storage of beer, and this was reached from the same staircase as the bedrooms.

The Mount in Hornton is a fine example of a three-unit farmhouse built in about 1680, and it is proof that the cross-passage plan remained popular to the end of the century in this part of the county, even for substantial houses. It is well constructed in tawny-brown ironstone, but is unusual in having the parlour isolated on the other side of the passage instead of the kitchen, an arrangement probably designed to give the parlour the best position next to the road. In this house the hall has not only been reduced to the size of the other rooms, but it has also to accommodate the staircase to the upper rooms making it clear that the parlour must always have been the principal family room. It is a comfortable house with three chimney-stacks and the quality of the masonry is excellent, with an especially fine label-mould with diamond-shaped stops over the main door.

We should, however, remember that most rural homes were of only one or two rooms, albeit usually now with a chimney-stack,

Carved label mould with diamond-shaped stops over the front door of the Mount, Hornton

and that the great bulk of farmworkers' cottages were generally still too poorly built to have survived from this period. In fact, most of the 'seventeenth-century cottages' advertised in estate agents' windows today were once the houses of prosperous yeoman farmers, although many had been subdivided in the eighteenth century when their owners moved out into more spacious homes. Blenheim Cottage at Brighthampton, near Standlake, is, however, a rare example of a tiny cottage that dates back at least to 1694, when it was sold by Nicholas Yateman Junior of Clanfield to the Churchwardens of Standlake for £32. It is a two-bay building of coursed limestone rubble and timber-frame with a thatched roof, and consisted originally of a living room and kitchen on the ground floor, and two small bedrooms on the first floor lit by a window in the gable and a dormer under the thatch. The only fireplace was in the living room, and we must envisage a whole family cooking and living in this one room. This is, however, typical of the housing of the great majority of Oxfordshire's population until the nineteenth century.

While the use of stone was becoming increasingly widespread in many country areas, timber-framing remained the main form of construction in the towns up to the late seventeenth century, though, sadly, most have been lost as a result of fire (made worse by the use of thatch for roofing) and redevelopment. Many builders no doubt preferred to use timber even for the grandest houses because it was cheaper than stone, it could be built high to give the maximum architectural effect on a small site and it could be carved and moulded to give a rich finish. In the seventeenth century this richness of ornamentation was often enhanced by the use of decorated plasterwork in the panels, known as pargeting.

A particularly fine example of an imposing house of this date in Oxford is the Old Palace in St Aldates which was constructed in 1622–8 as an addition to an earlier structure. Despite its constricted site, the building impresses the visitor by its height, being of three storeys with a jetty to both of the upper floors, and by the multiple gables along the skyline. The façade has been filled with numerous large and expensively glazed windows, which project from the wall supported on carved brackets, and the space in between them is decorated with fancy plaster pargeting, now much restored. The overall impression is of

abundance and richness, and this is continued in the interior decoration which still includes some fine plaster ceilings.

On a smaller scale, though no less elaborate, is the seventeenth-century frontage of 126 High Street, Oxford, which was added to a largely fifteenth-century building. Again we can see fancy carving, this time incorporating classical detail on the top floors, including an attic dormer with a small pediment over its roof and broken pediments to each side. Of particular interest on the façade are the large windows of exceptional quality. The first-floor window has glazing in the fashionable 'Ipswich Style', so-called after a window in the seventeenth-century Sparrowes House in Ipswich which has similar glazing with a round-headed central window.

Showy façades were not, however, limited to Oxford, and one of the most spectacular buildings in the centre of Banbury is the

Impressive gables and large glazed windows characterize the façade of the Old Palace in St Aldates, Oxford, built in 1622–8

Opposite: the façade of 126 High Street, Oxford, has large 'Ipswich style' windows of the seventeenth century (Print of 1880)

An
Old House
in "The High"
Oxford

This house in the High Street, Banbury, pictured here in 1884, was built in about 1650

very elaborate house in the High Street dated 1650. It is now a shop, but originally it was a town house of some importance. The three gables are decorated with carved bargeboards and finials, and below the two elaborate wooden friezes are three leaded bay windows facing the street.

Sadly these grand houses have mostly lost their rich interior decoration, which would have consisted of oak panelling or brightly coloured paintings. A rare exception is the Golden Cross

East St Helen's Street, Abingdon, in 1885, looking towards St Helen's church

Inn off Cornmarket Street in Oxford where a late sixteenth-century wall-painting still adorns a first-floor parlour, now used as a restaurant. The pattern is made up of pleasing interlaced designs, each of which contains a motif such as flowers or grapes, and it still retains something of the brilliance of its original colours.

Many less pretentious timber-framed houses than these can still be found in the streets of Oxfordshire towns, although sometimes only an old chimney or a sagging roof line betray the age of a structure that has been refaced in brick or stone in the eighteenth or nineteenth centuries. Often a glance from the back will reveal a much older building than the street frontage would lead one to expect. Some streets, however, still give us the feel of a medieval country town, such as East St Helens Street in Abingdon which contains many fine sixteenth and seventeenth-century timber-framed houses with steep gables and jettied upper floors. Here, large and small stand side by side, some replaced by brick houses in the Georgian period, but all now well cared for. We should not, however, be deceived by the fresh paintwork, for the great majority of sixteenth-century town dwellers lived in increasingly cramped and insanitary conditions as urban populations grew, and many towns became seriously over-crowded. Burgage plots were often subdivided and tall timber houses erected on very narrow pieces of land. In Oxford a row of jettied tenements that once occupied numbers 31 to 34 St Aldates was investigated by architectural historians prior to its demolition. These workers' homes were erected in the late sixteenth or early seventeenth centuries and consisted of one small room per floor, with a window to the street, and a chimney and adjacent newel staircase at the back. This block once housed several large families and was no doubt typical of many others that have long since disappeared from our towns.

A jettied town houses in Castle Street, Oxford (Twentieth-century water-colour)

4 The Georgian House

The Georgian sash-windowed double-depth house that is so familiar a sight in towns and villages today represented a clean break with the past and did not evolve from the types of houses we have been looking at so far. To understand this revolution in domestic architecture we must go back to the early seventeenth century when architects began to look with a fresh eye at both the design and the room plan of houses, and the inspiration again came from Italy. Here the work of Andrea Palladio served as a model for the application of classical styles to convenient domestic buildings, for, instead of adding fussy classical trimmings to essentially medieval buildings, he applied the proportions and geometric forms of surviving Roman public buildings to villas for the Venetian nobility, thus producing houses that were simple in form and symmetrical both internally and externally. Inigo Jones, Surveyor of Works to James I and Charles I, made a study tour of northern Italy and became the first English architect to appreciate classical architecture as a system of design rather than as a scheme of decoration, and his work at the Queen's House in Greenwich (1616) and the Banqueting House in Whitehall (1622) was highly influential. Both of these buildings, which have survived little altered, are externally plain almost to the point of austerity and their appeal relies on their symmetry, the pleasing proportions of their tall windows and the judiciously used cornices and balustrades. These buildings stand in striking contrast to the complex outlines and ornament of houses of the Jacobean era.

Palladio's villas may have inspired the return to classical forms, but in England it was to be the Dutch interpretation of the style that was to form the model for most late seventeenth-century country houses. During the period of the Civil War many members of the English nobility spent several years in exile on the Continent, especially in Holland, and after the Restoration many of them came home full of enthusiasm for the latest classical buildings they had seen. There was, however, already a house in England which united Jonesian principles with the latest fashions from the Continent. Coleshill House, near Faringdon, was designed by Roger Pratt in consultation with Inigo Jones and built between 1650 and 1662, though sadly it was gutted by fire in 1952 and subsequently demolished. The house was a plain, rectangular block with carefully spaced tall windows like Jones's other buildings, but Pratt also incorporated many Dutch features such as the hipped roof with pedimented dormer windows, the tall chimney-stacks and the octagonal roof cupola, which served both as a lookout and as an extra dining room for summer use. The façade was revolutionary enough, but contemporaries were even more impressed by the ground plan because this house was built to a double depth with a longitudinal corridor running from end to end. Unlike earlier

Coleshill House, Faringdon, completed in about 1662, was the first great classical house in Oxfordshire. It was destroyed by fire in 1952

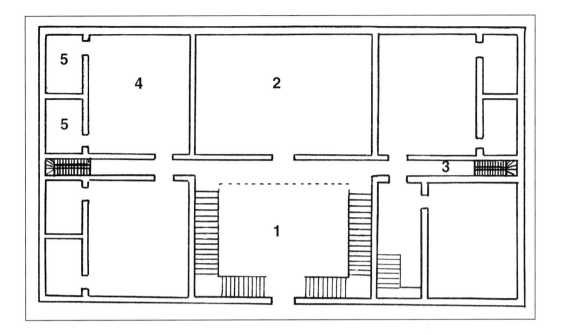

Plan of Coleshill House.
1 hall, 2 parlour (Great
Chamber above), 3 back
stairs, 4 chamber, 5 closets

house plans the interior arrangement was as symmetrical and logical as the exterior. A two-storey hall was placed in the centre of the house with the parlour opening directly from it, and the great chamber, or dining room, took up the prime position immediately above the parlour on the first floor. All the chief rooms were therefore placed in the centre of the house and this was expressed on the exterior by a wider spacing of the windows. The other rooms, arranged in mirror image on either side, could be reached from the main corridor and each was given two inner rooms or closets to allow flexibility in their use as bedrooms or parlours. The only place for the grand staircase was in the hall. This created an impressive approach to the dining room but made the hall unsuitable for use by the servants for meals, and they were therefore relegated to the basement rooms which further hastened their rapidly declining social status. Back stairs at the end of the corridors enabled them to reach the principal rooms of the house without having to use the main staircase, with the result that they were kept almost entirely hidden from view. The room arrangement at Coleshill was both practical and symmetrical, and it was to have a far-reaching influence on English house design.

Little new building took place during the Civil War, but after

the Restoration a number of houses were commissioned by returning members of the nobility, and, of course, they insisted on the Dutch Palladian style which was closely associated with Court tastes. One such builder was the Lord High Chancellor to Charles II, the Earl of Clarendon, who was granted Cornbury Park near Charlbury in 1661 and swiftly engaged Hugh May to design a new east wing for him. The style May adopted was derived directly from Dutch models and is very similar to Pratt's Coleshill, being of a plain block shape with tall windows, boldly projecting eaves and a hipped roof with dormer windows. Here, however, the eleven-bay façade was given a bold pedimented centrepiece and giant pilasters which emphasize the main rooms of the house and give it a striking dignity.

The east wing of Cornbury Park, Charlbury, was designed in the new classical style by Hugh May in the 1660s

Cornbury Park is not accessible to the public, but visitors can see an oustanding example of a major house of this period at Ashdown Park in the south-west of the county, now owned by the National Trust. It was built soon after the Civil War by the first Earl of Craven for Charles I's unlucky sister, Elizabeth, Queen of Bohemia. Sadly she died before its completion, but the house was survived almost unchanged and its pretty proportions express both its intended function as a hunting lodge and the desire for neatness and order in the years following the Civil War. It is a tall and narrow house of three storeys with an attic

and basement, and the style is in the Dutch taste with its hipped roof, tall chimneys and balustraded gallery on the top. The architect is unknown, but it may have been designed by William Winde who had been brought up among the exiled royalists in the Netherlands. It is constructed of locally quarried chalk with stone dressings, and a huge staircase with heavy balusters leads from the bottom of the house to the top. Perhaps its most endearing feature is the delightful cupola on the roof, intended as a belvedere for the owner to look out over the forest, with its wide avenues, which originally surrounded the house.

The new taste was at first very much confined to the Court circle in the early years of the Restoration, but, when Robert Huntingdon decided to rebuild his house at Stanton Harcourt in 1675, he adapted all the essential features of Coleshill and Ashdown Park to a relatively modest manor house. The house, now the parsonage, appears dignified and imposing with its tall rectangular façade grouped around a central doorway framed by Tuscan pilasters. The hipped roof, large chimney-stacks and dormer windows are in a pure Dutch style, and the tall, regular

Ashdown House was built in a charming Dutch style in the 1660s. It is owned by the National Trust, which has now removed the later pavilions from each side

windows give an impression of order and strength. Unusually, the windows have retained their original wooden mullion and transom crosses which in so many instances have been replaced at a later date by sashes.

While wealthy and well-educated men such as Robert Huntingdon were building in the Court taste, most builders in a conservative and rural county like Oxfordshire were content to perpetuate very traditional designs with their tall gables and long, mullioned windows. Occasionally, however, a local builder would attempt something rather more stylish, usually by taking a design from one of the many copy books then becoming available. A charming example is the Old Vicarage near the bottom of the High Street, Burford, which is dated 1672. The street frontage has been given a tall, compact look, with chamfered quoins at the corners to accentuate the

The Old Vicarage in the High Street, Burford, has unusual Dutch gables and the central one contains the date 1672 (Print of about 1900)

rectangular shape, but the curving Dutch gables on the skyline seem rather out of place, especially as they serve no useful purpose. Instead of framing dormer windows as one would expect, they are small in size and enclose blank, stone medallions. The first-floor windows are tall and elegant with their transoms and mullions, but those on the ground floor are long and squat, giving an overall impression of ungainliness rather than dignity. Nevertheless, the building certainly stands in contrast with the low and sprawling seventeenth-century cottages that surround it and would no doubt have been much admired by the citizens of Burford when first constructed.

By the turn of the century new influences were to oust the position of the Dutch taste in polite society. France, under Louis XIV, had become the most powerful country in Europe, and the splendour of the chateaux of Versailles and Vaux-le-Vicomte was legendary. Here, classical forms were being employed to create a sense of magnificence and strength, and giant columns, heavy cornices and curved walls had become the hallmark of a style often referred to as baroque. In England, in the years after the Restoration, while the yeoman farmer declined in status, the aristocracy had acquired an unprecedented degree of power and wealth and was eager to express its new confidence by constructing monumental country houses along the lines of those in France. It is particularly appropriate that the French baroque style was chosen by the Duke of Marlborough when, following his defeat of Louis XIV at the Battle of Blenheim in 1704, he was offered the royal

Blenheim Palace and its grand *cour d'honneur* (Eighteenth-century print)

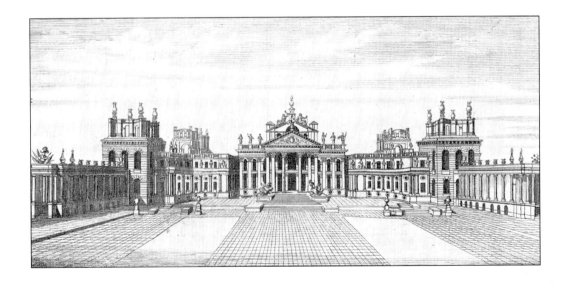

estate of Woodstock and almost unlimited funds by a grateful nation to construct a monument to his victory. John Vanbrugh was chosen as the architect, and, despite a series of conflicts with the redoubtable Sarah, Duchess of Marlborough, the building of Blenheim Palace proceeded with the assistance of Nicholas Hawksmoor and over 1,500 craftsmen and labourers. The result is a palace such as had never been built before, and George III, on seeing it for the first time, was quite overcome by its magnificence and was moved to exclaim, 'We have nothing to equal this.'

On entering the *cour d'honneur*, the visitor to Blenheim is surrounded on two sides by huge concave arcades and faced by a grand entrance through a portico of giant Corinthian columns supporting a pediment. The pediment reflects the formal centre of the house made up of the grand hall with the salon, or saloon (dining room), behind it, and the other parts of the house spread from here in diminishing importance to the service rooms and stables in the flanking pavilions to either side. Allied to the impression of grandeur is a sense of fortress-like strength, created by the solidity of the building with its square towers at the corners decorated with banded ashlar masonry and heavy brackets supporting the cornice. The monumental heaviness is to some extent relieved by the use of motifs, figures and 'eminencies' (as Hawksmoor referred to them), which decorate the skyline and add an almost theatrical touch.

The south front of Blenheim Palace in 1912. The heavy Baroque architecture was designed to give an impression of strength and grandeur

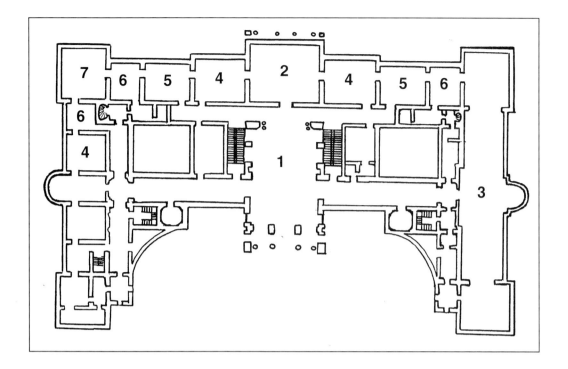

Of equal importance in the history of English domestic
architecture is the use of the French 'apartment' plan for the
interior, a plan that was first used in England in the seventeenth
century but which became almost standard for formal houses of
the early eighteenth century. We should remember that this was a
time of great social formality, when a strict etiquette in dress and
manners was seen as an essential reflection of the hierarchy of
society, headed by the sovereign and the aristocracy. The country
house of this period was not an escape from formality but an
embodiment of it, and every facet of its design was intended to
reinforce the social status of its owner and thus his political
power. Each apartment consisted of an enfilade of interconnected rooms without a corridor, and visitors were allowed to
proceed only as far as their status warranted: most of those
seeking jobs or favours would gain entry to the great hall where
they would be impressed by the soaring columns and Roman
arches, and some pursuing official business would be shown into
the Duke's ante-room. Visitors of higher rank would then
proceed to the drawing room or even the bedroom, but only a
few would see the Duke in his closet or 'cabinet' which was the
inner sanctum and the most intimate and lavishly decorated

Plan of Blenheim Palace.
1 hall, 2 saloon, 3 gallery,
4 ante-chamber,
5 withdrawing chamber,
6 bed chamber, 7 cabinet

rooms of the suite. The grandest apartments were the state rooms suitable for the accommodation of visiting dignitaries, and at Blenheim these were placed on either side of the saloon, while further apartments on the east side of the building were for family use. Apartments were provided in pairs for man and wife: they normally occupied separate rooms and etiquette was such that visits between the married couple were strictly regulated, which, in an age when most marriages were dynastic, often proved a convenient arrangement. Other apartments were placed on the first floor and were less richly decorated. There were thus few communal rooms except for the saloon and the gallery on the west side where the Duke's collection of pictures was displayed, for the design was intended to lay out an axis of honour to the great man rather than to provide rooms for informal gathering. This is often hard to imagine today because the bedrooms were moved upstairs in the nineteenth century, and the enfilades of state rooms have now lost their original functions and become a succession of apparently meaningless drawing rooms.

The magnificence of Blenheim is, of course, unrivalled, but the first half of the eighteenth century saw the construction of a number of major country houses in Oxfordshire. Heythrop House,

Heythrop House (Print of 1806)

near Enstone, built for Charles Talbot, Duke of Shrewsbury, is one of the grandest and was begun in about 1706. The baroque design is the work of Thomas Archer who had spent some time in Rome, and the bold use of sculptural detail echoes Italian work of this period. The room plan, centred on a two-storey hall, is similar to that of Blenheim, and so too is the emphasis on strength and grandeur, achieved here through the entrance portico of giant Corinthian columns and the use throughout of exaggerated keystones over the windows, banded rustication to the masonry and a strong balustrade at eaves level. Sadly the interior was destroyed by fire in 1831 and was refitted in the Victorian period. The building now serves as a training centre for a major bank.

English patrons never really felt easy with the baroque style, perhaps because its showy magnificence sat rather uncomfortably with their Whig protestant philosophy. James Gibbs urged a return to more restrained styles and was commissioned by George Lee, Second Earl of Lichfield, to design Ditchley Park near Charlbury, which is perhaps his most important country house. The façade is indeed plain, the only decoration being the quoins at the corners and the scroll brackets that support the window architraves, but the block is pleasing in its proportions with its projecting wings and separate service

Close-up of the strong sculptural detail at Heythrop House

Ditchely Park was designed by James Gibbs in the 1720s and marks a break with the Baroque style

The drawing room of
Ditchley Park in 1912

pavilions linked by curved corridors. The room plan follows the
now standard pattern of apartments centred around the hall and
saloon, and access to the principal rooms from the service pavilions
is provided by back stairs at each corner of the main block. In
contrast to the restrained exterior, the interior decoration is a
masterpiece of rich plasterwork and paintings created by William
Kent, Henry Flitcroft and three Italian artists in stucco. The huge
entrance hall, rising through two storeys, is a perfect cube and is
enhanced by plasterwork on the theme of learning, including
personifications of the arts and sciences reclining over the door and
overmantel pediments, and busts of literary worthies standing on
brackets adorned with garlands. The treatment of the adjacent
saloon is much lighter and freer, and indeed the flowing designs

The principal elevation of
Nuneham Park, built in the
mid-eighteenth century in
the Palladian style

The garden front at Nuneham Park has large Venetian windows to take advantage of the views over the Thames Valley

anticipate the exuberance of the Rococo style of the middle of the eighteenth century. Here, swirling scrolls frame a relief of Flora on the ceiling and a portrait medallion over the fireplace is surrounded by shells, scrolls and cherubs. Ditchley, with its rich room decoration within a relatively plain exterior, marks the beginning of a return to the 'Palladianism' of Inigo Jones which was to dominate architecture for the next fifty years.

Palladianism was an attempt to return to the strict principles of classical design by a new and careful study of Palladio's buildings, and it was made fashionable by the Earl of Burlington and the publication of Colin Campbell's book of engravings, the *Vitruvius Britannicus* (1715–25). The essential elements of the style included grouping the main apartments in a compact way around the hall and saloon on a lofty first floor (the 'piano nobile'), emphasizing the centre of the house by means of a portico or pediment, and siting the less important rooms on the ground floor which was to be of rusticated masonry cut to imitate massive blocks. In large houses the kitchens and other service rooms were accommodated in separate pavilions linked to the main building. There are a few houses in the county that were constructed to these principles, including Kirtlington Park, completed in 1746, Bletchingdon Park, remodelled in 1782, and Nuneham Park, built in 1756 for Simon, first Lord Harcourt.

Nuneham has been enlarged and altered several times since its completion, but the original seven-bay house was designed by Stiff Leadbetter of Eton as a compact Palladian villa, with the hall and saloon on the first floor approached by a double flight of steps, and the service rooms beneath. The house is, however, remarkable less for its architecture than for its situation, for Harcourt chose the site on high ground above the River Thames for its view over the domes and spires of Oxford which he believed would remind those brought up on a classical education of the view of Rome from the Campagna. Harcourt himself had travelled widely in Italy on the Grand Tour, and he was a founding member of the Dilettanti Society which sought to promote an interest in antiquity at home. The garden front was therefore provided with large Venetian windows taken directly from Palladio's designs to take maximum advantage of the views. This concern for a vista over a 'picturesque' landscape was very characteristic of the late eighteenth century, and it is not surprising that Harcourt brought in Lancelot 'Capability' Brown to improve the house and grounds in 1781.

Opening up the house to the natural pleasures of the park or garden became an increasing concern in the latter decades of the eighteenth century, when the main rooms were no longer placed on the first floor but were put instead on the ground floor with large windows facing directly onto the garden. This was in accordance with changing social attitudes, for the old formality of the first-floor apartments was no longer suited to a more fluid society with less formal manners. It was therefore abandoned in favour of a circuit of interconnecting reception rooms which could be used for informal reading, family conversation or entertaining. Drawing rooms, libraries, music rooms and breakfast rooms now made up the ground floor, while bedrooms were relegated to the upper floors and used less frequently during the day. In larger houses the library became the main living room, and in it a number of leisure activities could take place as well as reading. In her diary for 1778, Mrs Lybbe Powys described a visit she made to Middleton Park at Middleton Stoney. She commented particularly on the impressive seventy-foot library where

> besides a good collection of books there is every other kind of amusement, as billiard and other tables, and a few good pictures. As her ladyship is, according to fashion, a botanist, she has a pretty flower garden going out of the library.

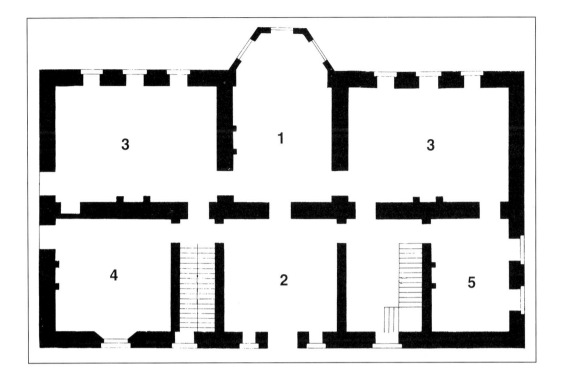

Because of its importance the library was often given the best position on the ground floor. This can be seen at Woodeaton House, near Islip, built for the banker John Weyland in 1775. A ground plan of the house, drawn by the author Arthur Young in the early years of the nineteenth century, clearly shows the library at the centre of the circuit of common rooms, with a canted bay window which looks out over naturally planted parkland.

Country houses had been built two rooms deep since Coleshill, but it was not until the middle of the eighteenth century that the double-depth or 'double-pile' plan became widely adopted for more modest houses. The single-depth lobby-entry plan was symmetrical but not very convenient as the central chimney-stack took up so much of the available space within the house. Thus dividing the stack and building it into each of the gable-end walls served to liberate the centre portion of the house. This then became the entrance hall with a central stair to the upper floors, and around it were placed four rooms: the living room and dining room at the front of the house, and the kitchen and pantry behind, with four bedrooms above. The double-pile house is therefore two rooms deep throughout, and is symmetrical with a central door and an

A ground-floor plan of Woodeaton House. New houses were now provided with a circuit of reception rooms instead of the old formal apartments.
1 library, 2 hall, 3 dining room, 4 breakfast room, 5 boudoir (Drawing by Arthur Young, 1813)

House in Steeple Aston in use as the village post office in about 1910. Most houses were built to a double depth from the eighteenth century onwards

equal number of windows to either side. For this reason it is often referred to by estate agents as 'double-fronted'. The plan allowed a framed staircase to be made a showpiece feature in the hall, for there was plenty of space and it could be seen as soon as the front door was entered. Farmers were soon building stout, double-fronted farmhouses away from the villages on the land they had recently enclosed, and the new design was taken up with alacrity in the towns where a more compact double-depth house was well suited to an urban situation.

The seventeenth century may have been the heyday of the yeoman farmer, but the Georgian period is one we readily associate with the development of Oxfordshire's towns. Merchants took advantage of the growing national economy and better communications, tradesmen set up shop to supply luxuries to the farmers made wealthy through their enclosures, and bankers and attorneys found their services much in demand. The new urban elites sought membership of what Oliver Goldsmith referred to as 'polite society', whose dress, tastes and way of life were established in London and Bath, and they demanded houses in the latest classical style to conform to the new standards in gentility. Within a few decades market towns such as Abingdon,

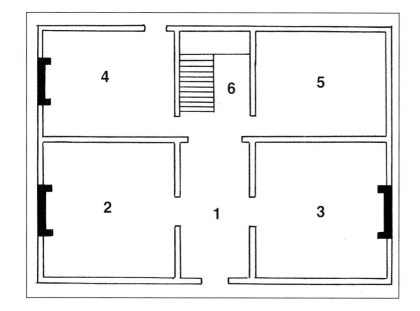

Double-pile plan: typical
room arrangement. 1 hall,
2 living room, 3 dining
room, 4 kitchen, 5 pantry,
6 stairs

Witney, Thame and Chipping Norton had been transformed by a
rash of rebuilding.

Local builders took the styles of the great houses and applied
them to the basic double-fronted house, with varying degrees of
success. Sometimes the full baroque ornament was applied to a
relatively modest house, such as the present Wesleyan Chapel in

Elegant façades in the High
Street, Thame, in 1904

Wantage. Country towns aspired to the latest standards in gentility and were soon transformed by a rash of rebuilding (Drawing of about 1810)

the High Street, Burford, which is reputed to have been designed by Francis Smith of Warwick in about 1715. Its fine ashlar masonry is of the highest quality, and the entire front is rusticated between the giant fluted pilasters to give it a monumental presence despite its small size. Originally the balustraded parapet was decorated with carved urns, before the

The Market Place, Chipping Norton, in the 1850s

The detail on this house (now the Wesleyan Chapel) in the High Street, Burford, is of the highest quality. It was reputedly designed by Francis Smith of Warwick in about 1715

building was converted into a chapel in 1849. More usually, however, town houses had plain and practical versions of the grand façades, giving them a handsome dignity. The former Judge's Lodging in St Giles Oxford, for example, was constructed in 1702 with a simple pediment to the centre three bays, and carving was restricted to the cornice and the cut quoins to the corners.

In the south of the county where good-quality stone was prohibitively expensive, brick became the most fashionable material in the eighteenth century and was often cut in the manner of stone. Architectural features such as pilasters, cornices and arched heads could be created from cut and 'rubbed' soft brick, and fine examples can be found in Abingdon, Henley and Wantage. Combinations of colours in the bricks produced by different degrees of firing were also used to give decorative effects in large houses, for example by picking out mouldings and window surrounds in red brick against a wall of bricks of a greyish colour. When Mr Ely built the Carswell in Abingdon in 1719 he gave it a semicircular well niche ornamented with a pediment and carved keystone, all carefully cut from soft, red brick. Successful commercial families were keen to erect houses as close as possible in style to the great country houses, and the Abingdon maltster, Benjamin Tomkins, was no exception. He built himself Twickenham House in East

Finely carved brickwork in
Ely's Conduit, Abingdon

St Helen's Street and ornamented the brick house with a three-
bay pediment, bold wooden cornices and a grand doorcase
made up of Ionic columns and a pediment containing a mask
and swags. Inside he created a large hall to contain a Chinese-
style Chippendale staircase. Other notable brick town houses
of this period include Calleva House in Wallingford, which
has a façade embellished with brick pilasters and a doorcase

Stratton House in Bath
Street, Abingdon, was built
in 1722 and displays some
fine brickwork

with a semicircular pediment, and Stratton House in Bath
Street, Abingdon, which also displays fine brickwork.

Fashionable town houses of the early to mid-eighteenth
century usually incorporate lavish exterior woodwork as well
as cut and gauged brickwork. The sash windows, which were
introduced from the Netherlands in the early years of the
century, were tall and narrow with wide wooden surrounds and
thick glazing bars, and the doorcases were often richly carved
with columns, Corinthian capitals and moulded pediments.
Sometimes hoods supported by scrolls or brackets were placed
over the door and the eaves were marked by heavy wooden
cornices with dentil decoration. Later in the century, however,
stricter building controls were introduced in London to keep
inflammable exterior woodwork to a minimum, and the
fashion soon changed throughout the country towards deeply
rebated windows and doors, brick parapets in place of wooden
cornices and much plainer doorways with fanlights above. The
architectural ornament of smaller houses is not, however,
always satisfactory in its proportions or execution, and this
was often the result of local craftsmen taking designs from the
numerous pattern books then becoming available. Sometimes
windows indicated in the pattern books were left unglazed
where they did not suit the needs of the owner, and these
'blank' windows have frequently been unjustly blamed on the
Window Tax.

The richly decorated
doorcase of Twickenham
House, East St Helen's
Street, Abingdon

Not all Georgian façades are what they seem. In many cases
old houses were refaced in brick or stone to fit in with their
neighbours, and timber-framed façades were given a rendering
of plaster and refitted with sash windows, taking care to
provide a tall parapet to hide irregular roof lines behind. Many
such frontages can be seen in the High Street in Oxford and
elsewhere, and the observer will notice that the sash windows

Exterior woodwork was
later reduced to a
minimum. This terrace,
Beaumont Buildings,
Oxford, dates from the
1820s

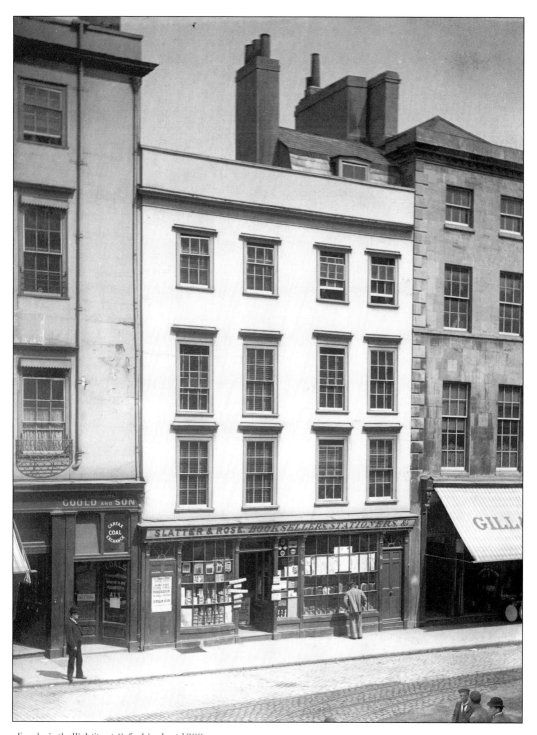

Façades in the High Street, Oxford, in about 1900

are of necessity almost flush to the thin skin of the façade rather than being rebated into a much thicker wall of brick or stone.

Of course it was not possible in old town centres to reproduce exactly the Palladian terraces that John Wood had used in his attempt to create the perfect classical city at Bath, where every spa visitor could share the refined surroundings previously enjoyed only by those living in Palladian mansions. However, in the early 1830s Beaumont Street in Oxford was laid out in imitation of the parades of Bath, though without the fine detail, and later in 1853 the Park Town estate was developed as matching crescents around an eliptical garden. But by this time the enthusiasm for Palladianism was fast fading, and the rest of North Oxford was subsequently developed in a very different style.

Beaumont Street, Oxford, was laid out in the 1830s on the site of the old Beaumont Palace. Notice the tramlines in this picture of 1908

5 The Worker's Home

We have seen little so far of the dwellings of the majority of the working population of Oxfordshire. Being mostly insubstantial they were frequently rebuilt, but from the eighteenth century the use of more permanent building materials has meant that many modest cottages have survived to become homes to modern families, albeit often knocked together to form larger units. Even so, houses built for the agricultural labourers who made up the core of the working population are rarely more than a hundred years old, most having succumbed long ago to rot or slum-

'Picturesque dilapidation': cottages at Little Stoke in 1895

Cottages in South Stoke in
1902. Rural life could be
damp and squalid

clearance schemes. The picture is a very diverse one in different parts of the county: money available to invest in building was greater in some areas than in others, and local building materials varied widely according to the geology and traditions of the area. It is worth considering each of these factors in turn.

Workers were generally worse off where they relied on incomes from the land because the days of prosperity for the small farmer or yeoman were long gone. Instead of rebuilding their farmhouses with style and panache as they had in the seventeenth century, many small farmers were now reduced to working for the large landlords who had the capital to buy up farms, enclose and improve the land, and raise livestock more efficiently. Large-scale enclosure schemes with the backing of Acts of Parliament were undertaken in Oxfordshire from 1758 to 1882, and they now took in not only the open fields, but also great tracts of 'unimproved' common land to be drained and hedged, often to the further impoverishment of the small farmers who used it to supplement their incomes. Sometimes this provoked violent disturbances involving the destruction of the new hedges and ditches, and the series of incidents that followed the enclosure of Otmoor to the north-east of Oxford in the early 1830s gained national notoriety for its bitterness. By the 1870s competition from imported grain and beef dramatically depressed produce prices and put further pressure on agricultural

Enjoying the summer sunshine outside a cottage on the edge of the graveyard of Dorchester Abbey in 1907

labourers, many of whom now abandoned the land to seek work in the fast-expanding towns. By the end of the century agricultural labourers in Oxfordshire were among the lowest paid in England.

Rural life was therefore hard for working people, and large families often had to be raised in cottages of only two or three rooms. Humble cottages were sometimes erected by the labourer himself on roadside verges or on pockets of common land, ownership being claimed as squatter's rights, but more often accommodation was provided by the employer as a tied cottage. In villages where there was no dominant landlord, rows of cottages were sometimes erected for rent by a local tradesman seeking an investment for his money, but in many areas there was little economic incentive to build in the hope of recouping the expenditure through rents; with labourers' wages at about 10s. a week, few tenants could afford to pay more than the average 2s. a week rent. Some workers were fortunate enough to be able to rent the old farmhouse belonging to a landlord who had built himself a new, more comfortable residence on newly improved land, or sometimes the old house was split up to house several families. But frequently the labouring family could

Humble timber and thatch
cottages, Long Wittenham,
in 1930

expect nothing more than an antiquated cottage on the estate.
Timber-framed cottages with deeply overhanging thatched
roofs may appear picturesque to us today, but a hundred years
ago most of them were squalid, cramped and insanitary, with
no facilities other than a village pump for water and a shared
privy. Old photographs convey something of the conditions,
but a picture of the interior of a typical two-roomed cottage in
neighbouring Wiltshire is graphically provided in words by
Richard Jefferies in *The Toilers of the Field* written in the
1880s:

> The chimney is placed at the end of the room set apart for
> daily use. There is no ceiling, nothing between the floor and
> the thatch and rafters, except perhaps at one end, where
> there is a kind of loft. The floor consists simply of the earth
> itself rammed down hard, or sometimes of rough pitching-
> stones, with large interstices between them. The furniture of
> this room is of the simplest description. A few chairs, a deal
> table, three or four shelves; and a cupboard, with a box or
> two in the corners, constitutes the whole . . . on the
> mantlepiece there is nearly sure to be a few ornaments in
> crockery, bought from some itinerant trader.

At least rural dwellers escaped some of the epidemics of disease suffered by their urban counterparts, but they were not entirely immune. On 5 February 1886 the *Berks and Oxon Advertiser* reported an investigation into an outbreak of measles in Cholsey, where the rapid spread of the disease was aided by the chronic overcrowding of a house in which five members of the family slept in one room and a lodger in the other. Nevertheless not all rural cottages were unhealthy slums, and Flora Thompson in *Lark Rise to Candleford* described a poor but wholesome life in Juniper Hill near Bicester in the 1880s: 'The inhabitants lived an open-air life; the cottages were kept clean by much scrubbing with soap and water, and doors and windows stood wide open when the weather permitted.'

The rural population of Oxfordshire was not wholly dependent on agricultural income, and standards of living varied markedly across the county. Before the Industrial Revolution had made its full impact, small-scale industrial pursuits were readily taken up to replace or supplement farm employment. In the north of the county fine textiles and 'plush' were produced in such villages as Adderbury and Bloxham, and in 1831 over five hundred men were employed weaving on their own looms within a twelve-mile radius of Banbury. The manufacture of leather goods brought work to other areas, particularly to Woodstock which specialized in gloves and to Burford whose fine saddlery gained a national reputation, while blanket-making became established around Witney. Many of the towns and villages in these and other parts of the county today contain stoutly built houses and rows of cottages erected to house a prosperous workforce in the eighteenth and early nineteenth centuries. However, they too eventually fell on hard times as coal-powered factory production in the towns made many rural occupations uneconomic, and by the end of the century most of rural Oxfordshire was in poor shape and little new building took place.

The internal appearance of surviving cottages has usually been altered out of all recognition in recent decades, but it is sometimes possible to reconstruct the layout and furnishings of the late nineteenth century from the memories of elderly people. Thatchers in Church Street, Bloxham, is a typical north Oxfordshire town house and its appearance in the 1880s was remembered by an old man whose grandmother lived and kept a sweet shop there. The house, built in the local ironstone, was then two dwellings that were entered by the same front door, and the present living room was divided into the kitchen and the sitting room of his grandmother's part of the house. The kitchen, the most used room, served as a combined kitchen, living room and sweet shop. It had an inglenook fireplace with seats, brass fender and fire irons, and in the centre of the room stood a round pedestal table with wooden chairs and a stool. The sitting room was used for 'best' and, besides a sofa and two armchairs, it was furnished with a chest of four drawers against one wall and a table with an American organ whose top could be removed for playing. Upstairs were two interconnected bedrooms, the stairs opening through a door into one of them, and they were furnished with iron beds, cane-seated chairs, two trunks for clothes, a chest of drawers and a washstand. Outside a range of sheds housed an earth closet, a coal store, a rack for killing pigs and various tools. This house, small as it seems to us, was not the smallest in Bloxham, for a number of poor cottages were cleared by the local authority in 1938, including a single-cell cottage occupied by Mr Mawle, a retired farm labourer, and his daughter. Mr Mawle's grandson remembered it as being a stone-built cottage with a thatched roof, consisting of a single living room lit by one window, with a small hallway and stairs passage cut from it, and two tiny interconnecting bedrooms upstairs. A dining table and chairs, a corner cupboard, a sofa and an armchair made up the furniture of the

Earl Harcourt moved his tenants into these new cottages in Nuneham Courtenay in the 1760s to allow him to demolish the old village which was in the way of his new park

living room, which had a stone-flagged floor, and the one fire had to serve for both cooking and heating. Lighting was by wall-mounted oil-lamps, water had to be fetched from a communal pump in Queen's Square, and the only lavatory, which served twenty-nine households, was also to be found in the square.

Accommodation provided by landlords did, however, vary considerably in quality, and many had motives other than profit. Back in the 1760s Earl Harcourt rebuilt the village of Nuneham Courtenay with stout chequer-brick semi-detached houses on either side of the Oxford Road, complete with a forge, inn, and curate's house. This must have represented a substantial improvement in living conditions for the tenants, but Earl Harcourt's prime concern was not the well-being of his workers but rather the opportunity to demolish the old village to allow him to create a classical landscape around his new house. Other landlords built with more philanthropic motives, including Lord Wantage who transformed his villages of Ardington and Lockinge in the 1860s through the construction of new cottages, roads, churches and schools for his tenants. The Bishop of Durham, owner of Mongewell village, was anxious to promote 'industry and sobriety' among his tenantry, and with this in mind he erected six pairs of cottages at a cost of £100 each, all provided with light, airy rooms, a garden for growing vegetables, and accommodation for pigs and bees. Despite the desirability of

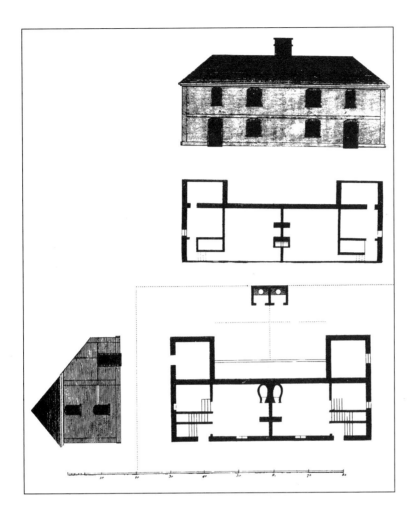

Plans for new cottages with outhouses at Mongewell, erected by the bishop of Durham for his tenants at a cost of £100 a pair

the cottages, he set the rents at two guineas per annum, much below the market rate, and in addition he set up a shop in the village to sell household goods at reduced prices. Providing good cottages and allotments for key workers was often seen as a way of retaining young people who may otherwise have sought to better themselves in the towns, and this was certainly uppermost in the mind of many farmers when they spent money on housing their tenants.

While underemployment and poverty were increasing their grip in the countryside, many towns were acquiring a wide range of industries in the railway age which offered wider horizons to young workers. Oxfordshire did not experience an explosion of industrial building on the scale of many parts of the country, but nevertheless Oxford and Banbury particularly were expanding

View of Cornmarket Street,
Oxford, looking north, in
August 1907

rapidly: Oxford grew from a city of 12,000 people at the
beginning of the nineteenth century to one of 46,000 by 1891.
New housing could not keep pace with the influx of immigrants,
many of whom were forced into overcrowded tenements or into
courts constructed on the long, narrow gardens of the old
burgage plots behind the street frontage. Most courts have now
been demolished, but we can gain some impression of their
squalor from old photographs and sketches, such as that of
Littlemore Court off St Aldates, Oxford. They were typically ill-
lit, overcrowded and poorly maintained, with facilities restricted
to a pump, wash-house and lavatories at one end. The authorities
took little interest until the cholera outbreaks of the nineteenth
century brought the squalor to everyone's attention; 86 people
died in Oxford in the outbreak of 1832, followed by 69 in 1849
and 115 in 1854. Official enquiries were soon set up to
investigate housing conditions in the city, and one of them
reported, for example, that in Jericho, 'a drain of the filthiest
kind runs . . . quite open . . . [there are] ten houses to one privy . . .
[and] a heap of vegetable matter in one corner', while another
deplored the conditions in many houses in St Thomas's and St
Ebbe's parishes. The population of St Thomas's was further
swelled from the 1840s by railway employees who crowded into
cheap lodgings and tenements where conditions became a

Littlemore Court off St
Aldates in 1923. Many of
Oxford's residents lived in
gloomy and insanitary
courts

Hollybush Row in 1906.
St Thomas's, near the
railway, was a particularly
poor and overcrowded
parish in Oxford

serious concern to the health authorities. Some parts of the city accommodated particular types of workers, such as Fisher Row on the riverside in Oxford which housed some of the many boatmen and their families who made their living on the river and canal. The 1841 Census was the first to give particulars of individuals, and, although many barge workers must have been away on Census night, we can find 18 canal boatmen, 3 bargemen and 6 fishermen and their families occupying a short row of tenements made up of old and new cottages.

In response to a growing awareness of the relationship between conditions of housing and public health, Boards of Health were established to enforce new building regulations and minimum standards of hygiene. Soon the immigrants were being housed not in narrow courts but in rows of brick terraced houses erected by small speculative builders. They mostly conformed to a fairly standard plan which in essence was half of the Georgian double-fronted design: instead of rooms to either side of a

Fisher Row, Oxford, in about 1900. These cottages on the riverside accommodated many of those who made their living on the Thames and on the Oxford Canal

Terrace of brick and slate
workers' homes in
Boxhedge Road, Banbury

central door, here there are two rooms, one behind the other, sometimes with a passage to one side to accommodate the stairs, and a yard behind with a privy. Often the business of daily living and eating was done around the fire in the back room, while the front room was kept for 'best' and little used.

The Causeway in Banbury is a good example of a terrace of urban industrial housing and was constructed by the developer William Wilkins over fifteen years between 1856 and 1871. The houses were built of locally made bricks with slate roofs, and consisted of a front room and kitchen on the ground floor, with a scullery built out behind, two bedrooms on the first floor and a separate lavatory in the garden. There is no entrance passage, and the stairs are placed in the kitchen and rise directly into the bedroom above. In the 1871 Census the tenants of numbers 57 to 129 The Causeway included a preponderance of labourers (22 per cent), brewery workers (17 per cent), foundry workers (18 per cent) and unskilled men, and 60 per cent of households were headed by a husband and wife, both of whom were immigrants to the town. Houses such as these were vastly superior to the dingy courts and tenements in the city centre, but accommodation was nevertheless cramped for large families, and thin party walls and other defects were not uncommon. Later in the century the standard of terraced housing for the artisan classes improved considerably, but poor sanitation remained a

problem, particularly in Oxford where many of the poorer suburbs were on low-lying ground and were subject to regular flooding and contamination of drinking water.

Late timber-framing at Letcombe Basset

We have seen that workers' homes of the eighteenth and nineteenth centuries vary enormously in their type and quality across the county, but there are other important differences too – in the materials used in their construction. Before the spread of the railway network brought cheap transportation of mass-produced building materials to all parts, cottages erected on a tight budget had to use local materials and traditional craft skills, and this means a great diversity in Oxfordshire where the geology is so complex. It is worth looking at each region in turn.

Timber-framing continued to be used for humble dwellings in the south and east of the county throughout the eighteenth century, but the thickness or scantling of the timbers continued to decline and the size of the panels in between increased. However, even poor-quality timbers were too expensive for many cottagers and they had to use a 'cob' of earth or chalk, though few have survived from before the nineteenth century. By this method, unbaked earth was raised in layers to form a stout wall up to a metre thick, often

Cob and thatch cottages in
Broadway Hill, Harwell, in
about 1900

with straw added to the mixture to give extra strength and to reduce
the problems of shrinkage. Each layer had to dry before the next
could be applied, so building in cob was no quick method. The
chief enemy of such a form of construction is damp, and for this
reason cob walls were generally set on a plinth of stone or brick,
perhaps tarred to repel water, and the top was given protection
from the rain by a deeply overhanging thatch roof. Cob is often
regarded as a primitive form of construction, but, in fact, where the
earth used is suitable, and not too prone to shrinkage, it could be a

Chalk, brick and thatch:
Craven Cottage, Uffington,
in 1916

Thatched Cottage in Wittenham Lane, Dorchester-on-Thames, has cob walls which probably date from the eighteenth century

highly satisfactory material. If the outer skin of fine clay or lime is maintained, the construction can remain weatherproof for a long time, however even a short period of neglect can allow a swift disintegration of the fabric. Once a cob wall starts to decay, it is very difficult to repair because the material shrinks as it dries and rarely forms a good bond, and therefore bricks or even concrete blocks have to be used to plug the gaps before the plaster render is applied. The observer can usually identify a cob cottage by the uneven bulging of the walls, which are often thicker at the bottom than at the top, and by the frequently deeply inset windows. One example of a cob house, possibly dating from the seventeenth century, survives at Wainhill near Chinnor. In Dorchester-on-Thames, Thatched Cottage in Wittenham Lane is a simple eighteenth-century construction with cob walls, a thatch roof and a brick chimney-stack in the gable. The method of building can be better inspected on garden boundary walls, which also had to be thatched for protection from the rain, and examples can be seen in Dorchester-on-Thames, Blewbury and elsewhere.

Sometimes it is possible to use soft chalk in blocks, though this poor building material was rarely used where alternatives were available. However, with the use of brick to protect the quoins and

window surrounds, it was possible to construct a serviceable house of this material, and the visitor to Uffington and other villages on the edge of the Berkshire Downs will find many examples of chalk and brick combinations. Some builders took advantage of the contrast in colour of the two materials to make decorative designs. In Woolstone, for instance, there is a cottage that is embellished with circles and diamond shapes inserted in stone over the main entrance, and in Dorchester-on-Thames one builder took this one stage further when he constructed Mollymops cottage in attractive alternating bands of brick, chalk and flint in 1701. More commonly, however, chalk was used as a rubble stone, and Ewelme, Benson, Watlington and neighbouring villages contain many eighteenth-century houses and cottages of chalk rubble with brick dressings. All these combinations, though vernacular and local, were seen as infinitely preferable to timber-framing which was now regarded as being very unfashionable.

Often associated with chalk is flint, and this could be used either knapped into roughly square blocks or coursed in its original nodule form. While the problem with chalk is that it is

The walls of these chalk cottages in Woolstone are embellished with circles and diamond-shaped inserts in stone

94

too soft, flint is by contrast very hard. It was difficult to cut with any precision or ease and therefore it too was usually employed in conjunction with brick, especially on corners and edges which cannot be formed in flint. This is especially so in the Chiltern Hills because there large quantities of flint were excavated in the nineteenth century as a by-product of clay digging for brick kilns, and cheap cottages for the workers were run up quickly using the flint waste and brick dressings.

The use of brick for small cottages was initially confined to certain areas where bricks were made locally, and brick-making was traditional in the Chiltern Hills from as early as the fifteenth century. This was not only because of the eminently suitable Marly clays to be found there, but also owing to the abundant beechwoods which provided cheap fuel for the kilns. The clays around Nettlebed were especially valued, and by the seventeenth century a number of kilns were being operated in this area by several families whose businesses can be traced through wills. The Sarney family, for instance, can be traced back to Robert Sarney who described himself as a brickmaker in his will of 1619, and it was still making bricks in the early twentieth century. Dr Robert Plot was most impressed when he visited

Chalk, brick and thatch make an attractive combination in these houses in Watlington

Flint walls with brick
dressings are characteristic
of cottages in the Chilterns

Nettlebed in the seventeenth century, and in his *Natural History
of Oxfordshire* (1676) he commented that the bricks made there
were 'so strong that whereas at most places they are unloaded by
hand, I have seen these shot out of a cart after the manner of
stones to mend the highways and yet none of them [are] broken'.

In the course of the eighteenth century the use of brick spread
across the county and also down the social scale as more kilns
were established. Bricks were rarely transported far for small
houses, and subtle variations in their hues of reds and oranges

Brick artisans' cottages,
Wantage

can often distinguish kiln from kiln and village from village. They were used initially as infilling or nogging for the walls of timber-framed buildings and for chimney-stacks, but brick soon became the automatic choice for rows of workers' cottages as well as for larger houses in an arc from Thame and Henley in the east to Wantage in the west, and from Banbury northwards. The demand for bricks rose significantly from the 1820s as the towns expanded, and by the 1880s some eighty-three brickyards were operating in Oxfordshire spread over all areas of the county.

Cottage brickwork is generally plain, with arched heads over the doors and small casement windows, but it sometimes contains some form of decoration such as a row of diagonally set bricks immediately under the eaves. Many local builders also gave their work an attractive chequer or diaper pattern by the inclusion of headers burnt to a silvery grey colour in the kiln. These were a speciality of the brickyards close to the Chilterns where the clay contains plenty of lime and no iron, and they were prized for their decorative qualities throughout the southern half of the county.

Most yards produced flat tiles as well as bricks, and these were used for roofing and also occasionally for vertical cladding in the south of the county where they helped to weatherproof exterior timber-framed walls. Tile-hanging never became as popular in Oxfordshire as in some parts of southern England, but

Brickwork could be given a decorative effect by the use of headers burnt to a silvery-grey colour in the kiln. This brickwork is in Beaumont Buildings, Oxford

Lime-plastered cottages with tile roofs, Steventon

Decorative tile-hanging on the gable of a house in Blewbury

examples can be found in Wantage, Blewbury and elsewhere, and it was sometimes given a decorative effect by hanging the tiles in diamond shapes or 'fish scales'. Hand-made plain tiles give character to an old roof or wall unmatched by their modern successors because they are irregular in form, having a camber in both their length and breadth, and they often display a multitude of variations in shades of red, orange and brown.

The use of brick can be found almost everywhere, but it never ousted the predominance of stone in the north and west of the county. Probably the finest stone came from Burford, and particularly from the famous Taynton quarries which supplied the builders of New College Oxford and Christopher Wren's London churches among others – indeed, the Kempster family of Burford supplied Wren with not only stone, but also a leading mason in Christopher Kempster. This limestone is soft when quarried and can be tooled with precisely cut detail, but it hardens with weathering and acquires the pleasant honey colour that helps to give Cotswold villages their particular charm. The cost of transporting the stone by river was, however, high, and builders in Oxford turned readily to stone from the Headington quarries in north Oxford as an alternative. By the eighteenth century the quarries covered some ninety acres and Headington stone was being widely employed as ashlar for buildings from colleges to rows of small cottages. Sadly the stone is not very durable as it blisters and crumbles easily with age, and many of

Oxford's buildings have had to be refaced with stone from Northamptonshire or elsewhere in recent decades. Cottages in the Oxford area were more often built of rubble stone, or 'coral rag', which was hard and difficult to cut and was therefore usually laid in courses giving rounded corners to the building. Window and door lintels were provided by timber beams and the roofs were of thatch. In the north of the county the ironstone quarried at Hornton and elsewhere is crumbly and unsuitable for fine detail, but it can be cut to form window and door surrounds, the remainder of the walls being constructed of coursed rubble. The tawny-brown colour of this stone gives villages such as Great Tew a picturesque warmth that is hard to equal anywhere, particularly when it is combined with a deeply overhanging thatch. Most stone houses were roofed with thatch, but from the seventeenth century onwards the village of Stonesfield to the west of Woodstock supplied builders in the Oxford area with 'Stonesfield slates' for roofing. The sandy limestone of this area

Leys Quarry, Long Hanborough, in about 1890. Many quarries were big business in the nineteenth century

Terrace of cottages, Yarnton, in the 1920s. Much of the rubble stone in the county is not suitable for making door and window lintels, so these had to be provided in timber; 'Stonesfield slate' is, however, excellent for roofing

Seventeenth-century cottages, Great Tew. The red ironstone of the north of the county can look very picturesque when combined with a thatched roof

is not naturally fissile like the Cotswold stone, but, by keeping it damp during the winter, it was possible to let the frost split it into thin layers suitable for roofing. By the nineteenth century the stone was being mined in large quantities and was used in various sizes, the largest being placed at the bottom of the roof and the smallest at the top.

Straw thatch was once a universal roofing material in both town and country, and many roofs that have since been tiled or stone-slated still retain the steep pitch that was essential to allow the original thatch to throw off the water. Long wheat straw was then abundant after the harvest, and it was laid onto the roof in bundles (yealms) and bent where necessary over ridges and dormers – indeed, the pleasing curves over 'swept' dormers are one of the most attractive features of a thatched roof. The ridge is usually given extra protection by a further thickness of straw, sometimes decorated by a variety of patterns made in the hazel

Steep thatched roofs at Weston-on-the-Green

spars securing it, and it is occasionally finished off by a bird or animal fashioned from spare straw. Owing to mechanical harvesting, long straw is now less easily obtained and non-native reeds are often used as a substitute. Reeds have a longer life span, but they are laid so that the butt rather than the length of the stalk forms the exposed surface and thus the appearance of the roof is very different. A thatched roof needs its ridge renewing regularly and its main slopes recoating occasionally, but underneath the original thatch can often remain undisturbed and may even be sooted from the smoke of a medieval open hall.

Roofs at East Hendred. Straw thatch was once the universal roofing material

6 A Return to the Past

By the third quarter of the nineteenth century the industrial production of building materials and their cheap transport by railway led to housing that was mass-produced, both in materials and design. It is not within the scope of this book to trace the development of urban planning into the twentieth century, but it is interesting to observe as an epilogue the revival in interest in medieval and vernacular styles that developed as a reaction against mass production. When the Norham Gardens estate in North Oxford was developed by St John's College from the 1860s, the architect, William Wilkinson, chose a flamboyant medieval Gothic style with gables, towers, pointed windows and tall chimneys. His intention was to recall the virtues of the

Victorian 'Gothic' style house in Norham Gardens, Oxford

Design for a 'Tudor' style
keeper's cottage at
Kirtlington Park (Drawing
by William Wilkinson)

medieval past, and the prosperous dons and tradesmen who
moved into these 'castles' were pleased to associate themselves
with their cathedral-building forebears. The quality and
traditional appeal of the past could be evoked in the small house
as well as the large, and William Wilkinson also designed the
Keeper's Lodge at Kirtlington Park with modern amenities but a
comfortably traditional Tudor exterior.

The Tudor period, readily associated with England's glory under Queen Elizabeth and William Shakespeare, was a popular choice of style in the late Victorian period. J.L. Pearson designed a church, parsonage and school at Freeland for the Taunton family during 1869–71, and he used a Tudor half-timbered style for the teacher's house – and it is indeed a tolerably convincing imitation at first glance as the materials and techniques were as far as possible honest to the original. Later, however, the imitations became progressively debased, and 'Tudor' semi-detached houses of the twentieth century use applied timberwork as little more than a surface decoration.

Recent decades have seen a new explosion of interest in buildings of the past. I hope that this interest will encourage more people to understand and appreciate the surviving old houses of our towns and villages, not only for the visual richness and individuality they bring, but also as tangible evidence of the daily lives of our ancestors, both rich and poor.

Schoolhouse at Freeland designed in 'Tudor' style, by J.L. Pearson in 1869–71

Picture Credits

The author and publisher wish to thank the following for their permission to reproduce the illustrations in this book (listed here according to page number):

County Archaeological Services (Oxfordshire County Council, Department of Leisure and Arts) 17, 37, 42

Oxford City Council, 97, 103

Oxfordshire Photographic Archive (Oxfordshire County Council, Department of Leisure and Arts) frontispiece, 1, 2, 5, 7, 14, 15, 19, 24, 26, 28–30, 32–35, 38, 41, 44, 46, 47, 50–1, 52, 54, 56, 58–60, 62, 64–5, 66, 69–72, 74–5, 83, 86–95, 98–102, 104

Mark Taylor 17

John Steane 37, 42

Select Bibliography

Airs, K. *The Buildings of Britain: Tudor and Jacobean*. Barrie & Jenkins, 1982.

Arkell, W.J. *Oxford Stone*. Faber, 1947.

Barley, M.W. *English Farmhouse and Cottage*. Routledge, 1961.

Beard, G. *The Work of John Vanbrugh*. Batsford, 1986.

Bond, J. et al. *Oxfordshire Brickmakers*. Oxford, Oxfordshire County Council, 1980.

Brown, R.J. *The English Country Cottage*. Hale, 1979.

Brunskill, R.W. *Illustrated Handbook of Vernacular Architecture*. London, (1978) Faber, 1978.

Brunskill, R.W. *Timber Building in Britain*. Gollancz, 1985.

Cave, L.F. *The Smaller English House*. Hale, 1981.

Clifton-Taylor, A. *English Stone Building*. Gollancz, 1983.

Clifton-Taylor, A. *The Pattern of English Building*. London, Faber, 1987.

Collier, W. *Historic Buildings: the Historic Architecture of the Thames Valley*. Oxford, Spur Books, 1973.

Cook, J. *Dorchester through the Ages*. Oxford University Department of Extramural Studies, 1985.

Cunnington, P. *How Old is Your House?* Alpha Books, 1982.

Fletcher, J. *Sutton Courtenay: History of a Thames-side Village*. Published privately, 1990.

Girouard, M. *Life in the English Country House*. London, Penguin, 1980.

Graham, M. *Images of Victorian Oxford*. Stroud, Alan Sutton, 1992.

Hoskins, W.G. *The Making of the English Landscape*. London, Penguin, 1970.

Jarvis, J. *Christopher Wren's Cotswold Masons*. Published privately, 1980.

Jessup, M. *A History of Oxfordshire*. Chichester, Phillimore, 1975.

Norwich, J.J. *The Architecture of Southern England*. London, Macmillan, 1985.

Oxoniensia. Journal published by the Oxfordshire Architectural and Historical Society, Oxford.

Paine, C. and Rhodes, J. *The Worker's Home: Small Houses in Oxfordshire through Three Centuries*. Oxford, Oxfordshire County Council, 1979.

Pevsner, N. *The Buildings of England: Berkshire*. London, Penguin, 1966.

Sherwood, J. and Pevsner, N. *The Buildings of England: Oxfordshire*. London, Penguin, 1974.

Watkin, D. *English Architecture: a Concise History*. Thames & Hudson, 1979.

Wood, M. *The English Mediaeval House*. Ferndale Books, 1981.

Wood-Jones, R. *Traditional Domestic Architecture in the Banbury Region*. Manchester, Manchester University Press, 1963.

Index

Page numbers in bold indicate illustrations.